S.

FOUND by Miss Charlie D.

Austin, TX

I found a book on the street called *Birth Without Violence*, which outlines techniques for easing the birth trauma and helping babies be born without pain, confusion or fear. This unusual contract, written on the back of a piece of flowery stationary, was tucked inside. I wonder if Mason's mom ever agreed to sign. —C.D.

I Deborah Parker agree not to punish my son ⊙ in any way for selling drugs to get needed soccer equipment and not to let my husband punish him either.

X _____

I mason mote agree not to get my mother involved if I get cought selling drugs.

X Mason Mote
_____

It is a strange life,
patterned in fire and letters
on the prison pavement.
—Hilda Doolittle

1

davy rothbart & jason bitner present

FOUND magazine

#5

THE CRIME ISSUE

This issue of *FOUND* is dedicated to Alexis Mazurin (1978-2005), pictured here with his sister, Nathalie. Alex was a passionate finder and a true *FOUND* champion who delighted in other people and helped recruit new finders far and wide. He is greatly missed.

FOR SALE STOLEN GOODS CALL: ROXANNE 2856814

Buffy — Call me on the Cell, I have documents about being in jail please call

FOUND #5

website by JASON BITNER

FOUND logo by Rob Doran

printed by Chris Young at WEST-CAN [866-337-1170 x.234]

additional drawings by TONY MILLIONAIRE · SARAH LOCKE · BRENDT RIOUX

made in Michigan · printed in Canada

COVER PHOTOS *FOUND* by Eric Michael Morris, Hammond, IN

REMORSELESS FOUND by Matt Sweeney & Kelly Neylon, San Jose, CA

CELL II CELL FOUND by Alexis Mazurin & Michelle Evers, Vancouver, B.C.

photos on the opposite page *FOUND* by L.M. Goebel, Indianapolis, IN; Pablo Rivera, Rock Springs, TX; Newt, Centralia, WA; Rob Lee, Norfolk, VA; Gordy Lawson, Portland, OR

label management by AL MCWILLIAMS at QUACK!MEDIA

c. 2007 FOUND Magazine & 21 Balloons Productions

CONTACT *FOUND* MAGAZINE!! info@foundmagazine.com

3455 Charing Cross Rd
Ann Arbor, MI 48108

Jud Laghi

Amanda Patten

DAVY'S POINT GUARD LETTER

What up y'all? Welcome to FOUND #5—the Crime Issue! Perhaps the finds we receive most often here at FOUND HQ—other than the "fuck-you-for-parking-here" notes—are letters to and from people in prison. There's always something about these letters that's really crushing, and a lot of times, there's something funny about them, too. More than anything, what emerges is a profound and transforming sense of what it would be like to be in their shoes. This issue has got several of these kinds of notes and letters, as well as a former FBI agent's life story, prison guard poetry, found notes about arson, pot, and self-amputation, academic crimes, crimes of the heart, found eyeballs, found crack, and the story of a guy who found a million dollars in the road. Enjoy!

Giant respect to all my friends who work so hard to keep FOUND running strong, especially Jason Bitner, Sarah Locke, James Molenda, Al McWilliams, and Brande Wix—their energy and generosity is astounding. Big big ups to the entire FOUND crew, and gigantic love to everyone who has become a part of the FOUND family by reading the magazine and helping to spread word about the project, and especially to those of you who've sent in finds—hell the fuck yeah—thank you, thank you, thank you.

Me and Popcorn Pete 'bout to jump in a van and come visit you! See ya in a minute. PEACE. —DAVY

DAVY ROTHBART
point guard, FOUND Magazine

FOUND
magazine
#5
STAFF PAGE

BRANDE WIX

JASON BITNER
power forward
FOUND Magazine

Shyel Meisels

Andy Schwegler
[Letterform]

April Glaser

Al McWilliams

Jordan Miller

Danielle Malkoff

Amanda Bullock

Timmy Smith

SARAH LOCKE

Kristin Halladay

David Wilcox

Nate Rogers

Eddie Faktorovitch

ARTHUR JONES

Javan Makhmali

Mike Kozura

JAMES MOLENDA

Jacob
Forster
Rothbart

David Meiklejohn

Josh Nussbaum

PETER ROTHBART

Andrew Cohn

007½

3

9/08/05

what's up lil bra
I been tryna call yo cell but
you probably didn't get that block off.
I need to get at u bout some
real shit. So when my mom
comes to visit find out so I
can let you know the special op
ya feel me. But they tryna to give
me a nice chunk of time.
I went to court and the
~~bitch-ass~~ judge was just about
to send me to YA ~~so~~ lil bra
I was fuck naw but my
lawyer ask for more time.
So now I go back to court
oct 17. It's looking real bad fo
me lil bra so I need to
take care of business while I'm
gone. But I betta not see you
in here. Try to stay out tha
town. ~~Niggaz~~ is dropping like
rain drops And I been hearing
all kind of shit so be
coo. Stay ahead of everybody and
get ~~···~~ yo money. I hope you

already took care of all that business I told you about. If not hurry up and get on that shit. Tell tito I know who did it. I already to you lil bra to tell him. Dube who did it got locked up but not fo that. Tell him I said I hope he gets well so and he betta start wearing a "life jacket." Feel me. But Ima let you go blood so be coo lil bra. Take care and keep ya head up. One luv

Big Bra
Bung

let me know what's going on. So write me. But when you write me the staff read my letters but you aint stupid let me know what happening.

AZZONE, JAMES
33;5-7;154;hr.blk;
ey.hz-blu;cp.dk;bd.m

YOU ARE UNDER ARREST FOR "CAR BLOCKING IN RESTAURANT!" (25 YEARS 1 MIL FINE!)

HOWEVER! DROP $200 AT MEKINNON'S WITH TOMMY & WE WILL CALL IT EVEN!! ASAP! COMMANDER "RORY" 248 470 74?

COP BLOCK FOUND by D. Hammond Northville, MI

SHELTER FOUND by Sean Robbins Phoenix, AZ

DID YOU KNOW? On Oct 15th 3pm- Andrew Will be arrested here @ work! NO Joke! :)

North Shore Animal League America is the world's largest no-kill animal adoption agency.

POST CARD

Hey Sis,
Lina is back in jail they arrested her the next day after the incident when I find out more I will let you know if you are interested I keep you and the boys in my prayers and I thank God for you everyday God Bless you always
Love Annette

NORTH SHORE ANIMAL LEAGUE AMERICA • PORT WASHINGTON, NY 11050

PC-16B4

GIVE A SHELTER PET A HOME — YOURS!

TO:

Mis

121

Ph

DID YOU KNOW? FOUND by Kelly Griffiths Burlington, VT

REAL HOPE

FOUND by Juli Pinsak

Ann Arbor, MI

I found this letter at the Ann Arbor Tech Center after it burned down, before the building was razed.

—J.P.

Dominique,

The only thing that matters in the messages you left me is that your mother has cancer, and that is terrible news. I have come to love your mom, and view her as Eli's real life guardian angel. She's been amazingly nice to me... kind and non-judgemental even after I got arrested, and through all the traumas of the last year and a half.

I can imagine the shock and dismay you and Brad must be feeling — but if anyone is a candidate for cancer survivor poster lady, it's your mom. Your dad and Pete are proof that there is real hope.

this photo FOUND by Juli Pinsak, Ann Arbor, MI

FOUND Magazine. No ink.

MOSES

FOUND by Matt Sweeney & Kelly Neylon

San Jose, CA

Anyone hiding my son Moses Reyes is going to be arrested! Reward & call

7

COLT Commando REVOLVER

Built on the same frame as the famous Colt Official Police Revolver that has a world-wide reputation for accuracy, ruggedness and safety. The Colt Commando is equipped with the-same features in war-time dress. Dull sand-blast finish eliminates all light reflection . . . stocks molded of attractive wood material. Featuring the Colt Positive Safety Lock that makes accidental discharge impossible, the Commando cannot be fired until the trigger is intentionally pulled. Sturdily constructed through-out, the Colt Commando is built for dependable action under all conditions.

MY LIFE AS A G MAN
THE MISADVENTURES OF ELMER L. JACOBSEN
FOUND by Eric Michael Morris   Hammond, IN

DAVY EXPLAINS!!

In a non-descript Dumpster in Northwest Indiana, FOUND operative Eric Morris discovered the vast files of a former FBI agent named Elmer L. Jacobsen. Between personal correspondence, mug shots, and newspaper clippings, Elmer's life story slowly emerges. It's an absorbing tale that spans decades, and includes Elmer's fight to end the waste of rubber bands, charged letters to and from J. Edgar Hoover, postcards from Iceland concerning a dead dog, kind boxers, angry stenographers, dapper criminals, bank heists, missing guns, and a cold December night spent lying in the dirt, staking out a restaurant in Council Bluffs, Iowa. Please read on.

We begin in 1937, with Elmer, at the age of 21, in college, working toward his dream of a life in the Bureau. Elmer's best friend, Johnny, who grew up with him in Minneapolis, has moved to L.A., where he's a promising young boxer. In a series of cheerful letters, Johnny recounts each of his prize fights, and encourages Elmer's interest in law enforcement.

Johnny Tachen, 1937

1338 N. Sultana
Ontario, California
October 15, 1937

Dear Elmer,
     The deadline you imposed on my answering is still two weeks away.
The penalty you set(receiving another letter from you) is a pleasant one
and not hard to take, but have decided will write sooner and hear from
you sooner as a result.
     If your plans for aiding the law-enforcement department of our
country go awry would suggest that you do your bit as a stool pigeon
as you seem to have one ear to the ground continually.(No offense-
I mean a very high class stool pigeon) Anyhow you make a swell
correspondent.
     If the two above mentioned professions don't fit, try news hounding,
or possibly you might be negotiator-in-chief of diplomatic-internation-
al relations. You do right well at complimenting. Outside of
     believe that this is the middle of October. Outside of
                              the same balmy weather we have had

8

*E*lmer is single-minded in his quest to become an FBI agent. He gets himself hired on at the Bureau as a file clerk, making $3.95 a day, and then in 1941, at age 25, he sends in this letter (below) with hopes of becoming a full-fledged Field Agent.

December 11, 1941

MR. GLAVIN

In view of the trying times that are ahead for this nation, and consequently this Bureau, I wish to apply for the position of Special Agent.

In furtherance of this application I bring to your attention these qualifications: Two complete years of a four-year night law school course in Minneapolis, 1935-1937; Ninety quarter-hour pre-legal credits at the University of Minnesota, 1937-1939; Finally, two and one-half years of law at Columbus University — upon entering on duty November 6, 1939, as a Bureau clerk. As for that clerkship — while employed as a Bureau clerk. I was assigned to the Identification Division until about July 15, 1940. This assignment included four months in the Messenger Room and five months in the Laboratory. Since July, 1940, I have been assigned to Personnel Files, the last four months as a clerical supervisor of the Midnight Shift. This Bureau background has been most beneficial and, I believe, will be an aid to good work in the Field.

For the past six or seven years it has been my ambition to become a Special Agent of the Federal Bureau of Investigation. During that period the appointment for which I am asking has been my sole goal. The long pursued LL.B. Degree was to be realized only if it did not conflict with that goal. So, even though my educational background is a bit chopped up, showing attendance at three different universities, it is only so because of the goal I seek. The first change—from law to pre-legal classes—came at the advise of Mr. T. D. Quinn in 1937 when I personally made application here and was interviewed by that gentleman. Of course, after the Minnesota pre-legal requirements were earned, it was back to the law and on with my ambition to become a Special Agent.

But, whatever the Bureau's decision as to passing on my qualifications, I shall willingly abide by it, continuing to pursue the LL.B. Degree while serving the Bureau to the best of my ability. However, I do feel that attending school cannot be reconciled with the Bureau's and the Nation's needs. All indications are that it is going to be a long, hard war; I wish to place my undivided efforts where they will do the most good—as Special Agent in the Federal Bureau of Investigation.

Respectfully,

Elmer L. Jacobsen

MY LIFE AS A G MAN
CONTINUES

March 21, 1942

MR. PATTERSON

On the morning of March 17th, the writer noticed quite a collection of clips and rubber bands in the box into which the char woman emptied all the waste material. This was at a time when she was little more than half way through her tour of Personnel Files. I asked her what was done with the trash material after it left Personnel Files. She was of the opinion that it was bagged up and destroyed. Then, curious to see how much was actually being lost, I requested her to leave her trash box with me when she left the Section so that I might examine it. She complied and I removed all rubber bands. They made an impressive pile.

The matter was brought to the attention of Mr. Gere and he suggested that I prepare this memorandum for you. After bringing the matter to Mr. Peeler's attention later that morning, it was decided that I should collect what valuable trash might find its way into the char woman's box during the balance of the week and then to report my findings to you.

I must say that since that first day I have noticed quite an improvement, especially in the case of rubber bands. However, this may mean that the 6 o'clock sweep in Personnel Files is catching more. But, whatever the reason I still have found a considerable amount of both rubber bands and clips and I can't help feeling that this organization, the FBI, could not possibly be as wasteful at work as the typical Government office.

Already much undesirable publicity has been broadcast nation-wide by radio and newspapers concerning extravagant government use of articles which have been denied the public market. I speak of the designation of aluminum and steel Venetian blinds in several of the new government buildings now under construction. Then there is the curiosity on the part of some newspapers as to what has happened to all the aluminum pots and pans contributed by "John Q Public". I believe that most Bureau employees feel as I do—that we do not want any dis-imization. Therefore, I suggest that arrangements be made to either stop all waste of materiel at its source, or to have some position approved such as "Salvager", or something to that effect, connected with the Char Force. This person would examine all trash for all items which should not be destroyed.

It might be argued that handling reclaimed clips and rubber bands would be rather dirty, but I think cleaning arrangements could be made. However, there must be places where slightly soiled rubber bands and clips could be used to advantage.

Respectfully,

Elmer L. Jacobsen

DEPARTMENT OF COMMERCE
BUREAU OF THE CENSUS
WASHINGTON

June 7, 1939

... to this Bureau by the Civil
... appointment to the position
... Washington, D. C. If you
... nature, probably of one or
... ory, and can in no event ex
... of the Sixteenth Decennia

... sition will be at the rat
... lent of $ 1440 per annum
... services justify advance

... nature, irregular or in
... r, and it is, therefor
... employment, and able
... census.

... promptly, please no
... cept employment if i
... report for duty, usin
...

... citizen of the Un
... this Bureau, and
... sh proof of natu

... but an inquiry
... lected.

... y truly yours,

Em

Chief, D

JOHN EDGAR HOOVER
DIRECTOR

Federal Bureau of Investigation
United States Department of Justice
Washington, D. C.

June 12, 1942

CC-240

PERSONAL AND CONFIDENTIAL

The Bureau is in receipt of the report of the physical examination afforded you at the United States Naval Hospital, Washington, D. C., on May 23, 1942.

This report reflects the following physical defects:

Flatfoot.
Slightly enlarged thyroid.

The Board of Examining Phys
recommendations:

Vaccination
Inocul

FOUND Magazine.
Examine all trash.

Elmer's advancement does not come easily. He toils as a clerk for another year, but even in his innovative approach to the conservation of office supplies, he displays blazing ambition. At last, Elmer realizes his lifelong dream—he's hired as a Special Agent and assigned to the FBI post in Birmingham, Alabama.

COLT

'Commando

REVOLVER

Caliber .38 Special

Trade Mark Registered, U.S. Patent Office

The bubble bursts almost immediately. Soon after arriving in Birmingham with his wife, Elmer commits an unimaginable boo-boo — he somehow loses his gun while on duty.

Birmingham, Alabama
March 17, 1943

MEMORANDUM FOR THE SAC:

RE: LOSS OF BUREAU COLT REVOLVER
NO. 684,979, ASSIGNED TO
SPECIAL AGENT ELMER L. JACOBSEN

Pursuant to paragraph 23, Section 2B of the Manual of Rules and Regulations, the following information is being submitted by the writer in connection with his loss of captioned firearm.

At 9 A.M. on March 15, 1943, the writer was assigned to the surveillance of Mr. and Mrs. Clyde Robertson, looking toward the apprehension of Nick Montos, in connection with Birmingham file 88-284, entitled GLENN DAVIS, with alias, Fugitive; NICK GEORGE MONTOS, with alias, Fugitive; C. B. PARSON, with alias, FUGITIVE, Unlawful Flight to Avoid Prosecution (Burglary), Knoxville being origin. Montos is the last of the three subjects at large and is known to be the most dangerous. Accordingly, the writer wore his sidearm.

The writer accompanied Special Agent James W. Campbell, to whom instant case is assigned, in one car until about 11 A.M., at which time Special Agent James Douglas Allen joined the surveillance with a second car. From this point on the writer continually changed cars as expediency dictated. There was need for two cars in this case inasmuch as Mr. and Mrs. Robertson each had a car, and it was known that they were acting as Montos' mail drop. They also were known to be in possession of a letter from Montos' sister in Tampa, Florida, which had been addressed to their address and to the alias of Montos, J. S. Rosen. One of the Robertsons was expected to forward this letter to Montos. If the letter were not forwarded, it would possibly mean that Montos was actually a resident in the Robertson home or was soon expected to be. The writer's duty was to watch Clyde Robertson's every action until the letter was mailed and then to stand over the mail box until a postman arrived.

The Robertsons' house at 506 Manchester Lane, Homewood, Alabama, a suburb of Birmingham, was the base of our operation. This house is peculiarly situated so as to make it necessary to view it from a distance of some sixth of a mile through a grove of trees. It was impractical to be closer. The hills amongst which this house was situated contain a maze of roads, which gave the Robertsons six avenues by which to leave and in which a surveillance-conscious individual could immediately lose a would-be surveillant unless the latter showed the utmost speed and foresight after viewing the surveilled's initial move. The two Bureau automobiles were parked facing in opposite direction, and the writer would accompany the driver

Forget the FBI!
Track us down yourself—
info@foundmagazine.com

3455 charing cross • ann arbor, mi • 48108

11

MY LIFE AS A G MAN CONTINUES ➞

facing in the proper direction when one of the Robertsons left the residence. Inasmuch as Robertson had made some sudden stops and sudden "U" turns on the writer and accompanying Agents that morning, it was more than ever apparent that great speed - of mind, feet, and car, would be necessary to keep either of the Robertsons within sight throughout the afternoon. After several unsuccessful attempts in the morning to give the above mentioned Agents the "slip," Robertson again left his house about 1:00 P.M. At this time the writer knew he still was in possession of his firearm inasmuch as he had assured himself of that fact as he ate his lunch in the car while maintaining the surveillance.

Throughout the afternoon the writer was intermittently in need of hurriedly entering and leaving one or the other car. These movements were preceded by periods of watchful waiting in one of the cars, during which time the writer's firearm could possibly have worked itself loose from the holster against the upholstery of the car.

The writer has since tried sitting in a car, both with and without a revolver in the holster, and could feel little difference. Therefore, he does not believe that there was any negligence on his part in not feeling that the gun was gone. All action outside of the cars was of such nature that the writer did not have occasion to think about the weight missing from his hip. Twice it was necessary for the car to be left empty and unlocked to avoid suspicion. Neither time was for more than five minutes.

The firearm was first noted to be missing about 6 P.M. on February 15, 1943, whereupon the writer immediately conducted a thorough search of both cars used and the ground traversed during that afternoon.

To secure the return of this gun, the following steps also have been taken:

At the Birmingham Police Department the gun has been registered under the writer's name and address as being either lost or stolen. The pawn shops in Birmingham are in the practice of daily reporting to the Police Department guns received. The Wednesday, March 17, 1943, Birmingham papers are carrying the writer's advertisement in the Lost and Found column with orders to continue the ad through Sunday, March 21, 1943. This ad reads as follows:

"Revolver. .38 caliber Colt, blue steel, lost Monday. Reward. Phone 4-3772."

The Bureau is hereby assured that it will not be embarrassed in any way concerning this episode. All inquiries in investigations that the writer has made concerning this sidearm have been made in a discreet and tactful manner. Mrs. Jacobsen will be handling all telephone inquiries in a similar manner and keeping the Bureau's name out of this matter.

-3-

The writer can only assure that he was attending strictly to business and intent on giving his best efforts to the case at hand when this loss occurred. He, of course, deeply regrets that this misfortune had to occur but does not feel that under the circumstances, which demanded speed and agility, he was at all negligent. However, he does feel that an improvement of his perspective and knowledge of the limitations of the standard holster will follow from this bitter experience.

Respectfully submitted,

ELMER L. JACOBSEN,
Special Agent

HOOVER, J. EDGAR (1895-1972), served as director of the Federal Bureau of Investigation (FBI) for 48 years. He held the office from 1924 until his death. Hoover built the FBI into one of the world's outstanding law-enforcement agencies. However, a congressional investigation after his death raised questions about some of his actions.

J. Edgar Hoover

Boss-man is pissed!

JOHN EDGAR HOOVER
DIRECTOR

Federal Bureau of Investigation
United States Department of Justice
Washington, D. C.

March 29, 1943

Mr. Elmer L. Jacobsen
Federal Bureau of Investigation
United States Department of Justice
Post Office Box 314
Birmingham, Alabama

Dear Sir:

The Bureau has been informed of the loss of your revolver Number 684979 while recently assigned to a surveillance and I am writing to advise you of my extreme displeasure over the entire incident. All Special Agents of this Bureau are cognizant of the fact that due precaution should be taken at all times to safeguard Bureau property, and your carelessness in neglecting to take proper precaution is considered inexcusable.

In view of your negligence in this instance, you are being suspended without pay from 9 A. M. March 31, 1943 to the close of business April 9, 1943. Further derelictions on your part will result in more severe disciplinary action.

It is requested that you submit a check in the amount of $28.91 in payment for the revolver. This check should be made payable to the United States Treasury, Washington, D. C.

Very truly yours,

J. Ea. Hoover

John Edgar Hoover
Director

FOR VICTORY
BUY
UNITED
STATES
DEFENSE
BONDS
AND
STAMPS

Unfortunately, for Elmer Jacobsen, the trouble was just beginning...

MY LIFE AS A G MAN **CONTINUES ON PAGE** 25

INHERITANCE
FOUND by Laura Cavaluzzo
San Francisco, CA

I, Becka McNeil
State herein that
Upon my death
Drew Keel has
all legal rifes to
my skull

FAT ASS SKULL
FOUND by Jeremy Smith
Holyoke, MA

Fat ass!

HARD OUT HERE
FOUND by Chris Rivera
Las Cruces, NM

While helping a friend clean out an apartment he was moving into, I found this Grand Jury subpoena with a truncated letter on the back, along with some hasty math.

—C.R.

Dear Babe
        You are probably wondering
why I didnt go see you, but it is
hard out here to do things when I
have no one to

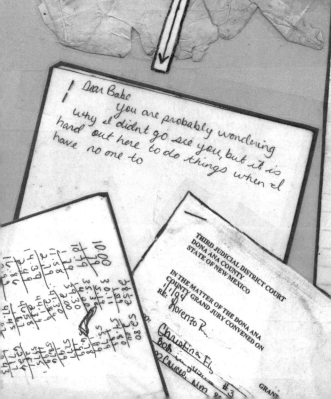

THIRD JUDICIAL DISTRICT COURT
DONA ANA COUNTY
STATE OF NEW MEXICO

IN THE MATTER OF THE DONA ANA
COUNTY GRAND JURY CONVENED ON
11/04

RE:
Florenzo R.

Carolina El.
Bob
Cruces, Nm

CHAPTER 13
FOUND by Eric Snow
Cleveland Heights, OH

I got another Lab bill for $376 dollars. I gave that one to her and she just started laughing. You know as long as I am Here, they have to pay all of my doctor bills. So me and her was thinking thats about 4 or 5 thousand dollars in doctor bills already.

Anyway, if things dont work out that way, there was a lady in Here the other day and we was talking and she told me that she was in here for the same thing I # an (checks) but the only reason she was Here was a paperwork error. She told me that I should look into filing bankruptcy because thats what she did and she had $32,000 thousand dollars worth of bad checks and she has not spent one night in jail because some body told her about chapter 13 and she put all of that on her bankruptcy and the courts cant touch her because once she filled she can only make payments on her bankruptcy and not to the courts anymore. She gave me the name of the man she used and

SMOKIN' THE DOUGH

FOUND by Johnny Vo
Los Angeles, CA

In my neighborhood, there's always gang kids hanging out smoking pot and drinking 40's after school. One day I saw two cops grab a kid, put him in handcuffs, and throw him in the back of their squad car. After they took off, I found this note, which the kid must've dropped when he was arrested. I think he was the one who wrote it.

—J.V.

II: MI COOKIE MONSTER
IM SORRY ON HOW I'M ACTING. BUT I WANT TO LET YOU KNOW THAT I GOT MAD 4 A REASON. CUZ LATELY GIRL YOU'VE BEEN FUCKING UP. I CARE ABOUT U GIRL I DONT WANNA SEE YOU FUCK UP. U EVEN SAID YOU DONT WANNA. DO IT FOR YOUR FRIENDS OR DO IT FOR YOUR CUZ ¿ GRANDMA OK. CUZ LOTZ OF PEOPLE CARE ABOUT U. IF YOUR NOT GOING TO LISTEN THEN DO WHAT U THINK ITS RIGHT. LIKE U SAID Y U R GOING TO BE BLAZIN OR DITCHIN JUST SO U COULD THINK UR THE SHIT. I KNOW UR SMART SO DONT BE USING UR DUMB SIDE. K. WRITE BACK OR CALL ME. MERRY CHRISTMAS ¿ HAPPY NEW YEAR. LOVE YOU. 4RM: YOUR GROUCH.
BARRIO SESAME STREET

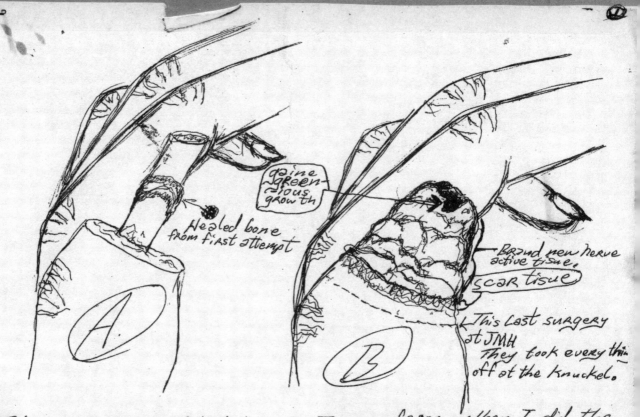

gaine green-ious grow th

Healed bone from first attempt

A.

Brand new nerve active tisue.

scar tisue

This Last surgery st JMH They took every thi off at the knuckel.

B

It was ~~around~~ feb. but maybe January of 2001, when I did the first ~~anithisal~~ attempt of cutting off my Left first finger in which my physical therpist richard insisted me to go to the emergency room or he wasn't going to accept me for therapy anymore. I went to the emergency room, they ended up sowing the finger back on. In which I wasn't able to straten the finger or curel as normaly. Well over a month latter I realized my finger wasn't getting better around march the 2 y th I decided I would be botter to take the finger all the way off. But this time make sure the machetie makes it all the way through set I cut the finger all the way off this time, but I missed the nerves (stiched) (healed) spot that was limiting the fingers fhatom movement still. nerve So after 4 days of (at) trying to work out the fhatom Limitation, tendon I decided to cut ~~off~~ ~~the~~ down to where the nerve was severed the first time. I sharpened my pocket knife almost razor sharp & made bone deep cuts around the finger, Just above the nuckel. This got the fhatom Limitation out. So I could now Imagine the finger stratening out & curling completly. I did the same process that I did with the dogs neck, I took yuca fibers wraped them around the bone then wraped the hand with a vary airy cloth so to get plenty of air flow to the wound A in 1½ weeks actualy about 8 or 9 days I had (got) over an inch of brand new completly nerve active tisue growth. The only reason (I came to JM H) or I was about to come to JMH is because the bone end peice had broke loose & I pulled it out of the tisue mass. This gave wey for Bone marrow

Blood (which has no antibiotics at all) to come out & mix with the
This also backs up my understanding of this blood being able to become any
promote
specificly Nerve cell growth structure
the ~~Bo~~ small amount of Bacteria which is needed to keep the body
putting out white blood cells. This blood was extreamly good food for
the bacterias growth of whatever it could acheve which was ~~is~~ going green
the strongest form of bacterial growth. I didn't want to have to
deal with the pain again & at the same time share some vary benifical
Knowlage with the world of mankind. But the person I confided in
Help with
for some (aid in) sending this information to ~~GARY LOHR of vanoasdale 444-6625~~ news centers so I'd
have some backing when going to (JMH) instead called 911.

What has happened & is happening is exactly why I
wanted to have some ~~~~Right backing me up before I came to
JM Hospital.

The doctors are trying to say this new tissue growth
was scar & or gongulation tissue. First thing right off the bat
scar or gongulation tissue can't grow to this digree outside of the
Body & it wouldn't be nerve active or have blood flowing through
it. This tissue not only had plenty of circulation but it had
vary Recognizable nerve sensation throughout all surfface area,
& at the end where the goine green ended up being, their was
3 maybe 4 spots that looked like a pencial graffite stab wound
even
but when tuched with a supper ~~soft~~ flexable plant fiber it
brand new
sent an electrical shock to my brain as if putting a 9v battery
on your tounge.

That shows their was good NERVE response
& sensation throughout the complet ~~tissue~~ coverage

TO THE LOVE OF MY LIFE! MY LOVELY WIFE... AURIA I LOVE YOU FOREVER AND A DAY. ALWAYS YOUR HUSBAND. ME, ADRIAN/B. LOVE'S AURIA

I LOVE JEW MAMDTA MIA

AB & AB UNTIL

HEY BABY   FOUND by Fred van Vector

Eugene, OR
at the corner of 13th & Pearl

Hey Baby,
Oh my gosh do I miss you! I want to be with you so so bad. I can't wait until your next to me again! I can't wait until I get to touch you again! When you get out I'm making you stay in bed w/me all day long! I can't wait until I can make love w/you again I would give anything to be able to make love to you right now! If only you were here I wouldn't let you leave my bed. I miss you so so much! I just wish I could have you right now!! What do you wish we could we be doing right now? I've just been thinking about all the things we've done together and in the 15 months we've been kind of dating what we have done together! I miss having sex with you! do know that do you know how much I miss feeling your body against mine. you touching me and rubbing me!! I loved seeing you naked! anytime I

was around you all I wanted to do was have sex w/you! thats all I could think of all day long when you were working I would wait and wait for you to come home so I could have you! I loved when you slept naked. I wish you always slept naked Do you think you can when we live togeth again? I would do anything to have you again right now. Baby I love you! I thought maybe my feelings might have been changing but they aren't I loved when you would put your arms around me on my boob you would rub my legs and arms back butt I would do anything to have you do that again. I can't wait for the day you get out! It well be the best ever! can you wait! If we could have sex now would you? I ♥ u! do you get how much I want you? how much I miss + love you? I hope so. I want us to get married now. I want to have a huge wedding ask me again to marry you I hope you still want to get married

7-23-95
I
LOVE
YOU
HONEY!
YOUR
SO
SPECIAL
AND
FOREVER
WILL BE
LOVEN
YOU.
TU MARIDO
ADRIAN.B
♡
AURIA.B
PARA SIEMPRE

these photos FOUND by Devin Friedman, New York, NY

8-27-95

REAL ROCK FROM THE ROCK

FOUND by Rick Callaway Seattle, WA

I found this note — written on a Jail Health Services form — on a wet downtown sidewalk. —R.C.

Throw Rock in water — Give her a Rock

Ask her what she see's Then tell her that she is the Rock and that ripples are what happend to me when you came into my life 5 years ago Nikki like the Ripples in the water I want the Rest of our lives to be a series of Ripples That last a lifetime.

Nikki Alexandria Hendrickson would you

Do me the honor and make me the happiest

man on Earth and be my wife; will you

MARRY ME?

INSIDE

OUTSIDE OF NOTE

FOR MY WIFE

Medical Kite – Health Request

Public Health
Seattle & King County
HEALTHY PEOPLE. HEALTHY COMMUNITIES.
Jail Health Services   Jail Health Services
500 Fifth Avenue   620 West James Street
Seattle, WA 98104   Kent, WA 98032

DAJD F-538 Back (12/05)

Patient Name
BA #:
D.O.B.:

FOUND Magazine. A series of ripples.

19

MESC 1707
(REV. 4-93)

DEPARTMENT OF LABOR
MICHIGAN EMPLOYMENT SECURITY COMMISSION
REQUEST FOR INFORMATION RELATIVE TO POSSIBLE INELIGIBILITY OR DISQUALIFICATION
Authorized by MCl 421.1 et seq

B.O. No. ....

TIMOTHY
1479 ████████ NE APT A
GRAND RAPIDS MI 49505-5365

CLAIMANT:
377-94-28
TIMOTH

PLEASE RETURN FORM TO:
MESC B.O.   043
3391 PLAINFIELD NE
GRAND RAPIDS   MI   4950

PHONE NO: (616)361-3200
FAX NO: (616)361-3229

This unemployment claim has a potential qualification/eligibility issue and is being investigated to determine w benefit entitlement, if any, the claimant has. Please answer the specific question(s) listed below which are ba on the claimant's and/or employer's statement. Please submit all pertinent information which you believe would helpful in the proper disposition of the issue(s) involved. If necessary, use an additional sheet of paper to subm that information.

You are required to complete this form within 10 days whether you feel payment(s) on this claim should be allo or denied. If a reply is not received within 10 days, a determination will be made on the basis of the available fa You should retain a copy of this form for your records.

YOUR EMPLOYER HAS NOT INDICATED THAT SHORTAGES WAS YOUR REASON FOR DISCHARGE. STATED YOU PLAYED WITH MATCHES AND SET FIRE TO PAPER IN A TRASH CAN. SET FIRE TO REPORTS. WROTE ABSCENE GRAFFITI ON THE PAPER WORK. CALENDARS AND POSTED SIGNS. YOU ENGAGED IN HOURSEPLAY- POURING AMMONIA ON DRY ICE IN THE BACK ROOM WHICH CAUSED THE DRY ICE TO EXPLODE. YOU TWIRLED A BROOM AND HIT A CUSTOMER IN THE HEAD.

Mailed Month   11   Day   12   Year   96   Claims Examiner   B HARTLINE

Claimant's First Day Worked: _____   REPLY

_____ Last Day Worked: _____

_____ Date of Removal From Payroll: _____

FOUND Magazine twirled a broom and hit a customer in the head.

NEW RELEASES
FROM
21 BALLOONS
PRODUCTIONS

The Sight
of Any Bird

The   Poem   Adept

The Poem Adept
The Sight
of Any Bird

ANVIL.
NEW MUSIC FOR
VIRTUOSOS

NEW MUSIC FOR
VIRTUOSOS

ANVIL

21balloons.com

21IBP-002
2 CD SET

Davy Rothbart
THIS AMERICAN LIFE

This
American
Life
from WBEZ CHICAGO

Davy Rothbart
THIS AMERICAN LIFE

Davy Rothbart
THIS AMERICAN LIFE

Ghost Da...
Jets

Disc One

1. Mr. Rogers and Me
2. Who NeedsTwo?
3. Lost in America

21

VISIT US!
MYSPACE.COM/21BALLOONS
21BALLOONS.COM

this photo FOUND by Rob Elder, Ronkonkoma, NY

UNDIGNIFIED PLEADING

FOUND by Davy Rothbart

Ypsilanti, MI

From: Walter Gerald
Date: Dec 18, 2006 4:57 PM
Subject: Re: final
To: Andrew

Andrew,

I have not graded your test yet, but it is clear that my message to you about receiving the grade you earn has not gotten through. To write, as you do, "Please have mercy on my soul and give me a passing grade. I think I deserve it," indicates that, as do your numerous pleas for mercy earlier in the course. Grading is about receiving what your coursework indicates you deserve. Nothing else!! I have operated on that principle for about 40 years, and I am not about to change now. So please stop the undignified pleading. I'll enter the grades for all the students in 344 at the same time, and you will ALL receive what you EARN. No more, no less.

WM

----- Original Message -----
From: Andrew
Date: Monday, December 18, 2006 12:32 pm
Subject: final

[Hide Quoted Text]

--
Andrew P-

cal   - missing work

① *Five People you meet in Heaven due: 9/21/06

②

This paper is very late and can no longer be turned in and has resulted in an "F".

Thank you!

ONE TEACHER YOU MEET IN HELL

FOUND by Molly McGillicuddy's class
Our Lady of Nazareth H.S
Wakefield, MA

FOUND Magazine.
No more. No less.

LET'S GET FREE

FOUND by George Ponnovich
Lockport, IL

I work in a state prison outside of Chicago. I was walking in the solitary confinement unit a few years ago and found this escape plan. It made me laugh because it's so simple. I asked the inmate when he was going to carry this out. His response was unprintable. —G.P.

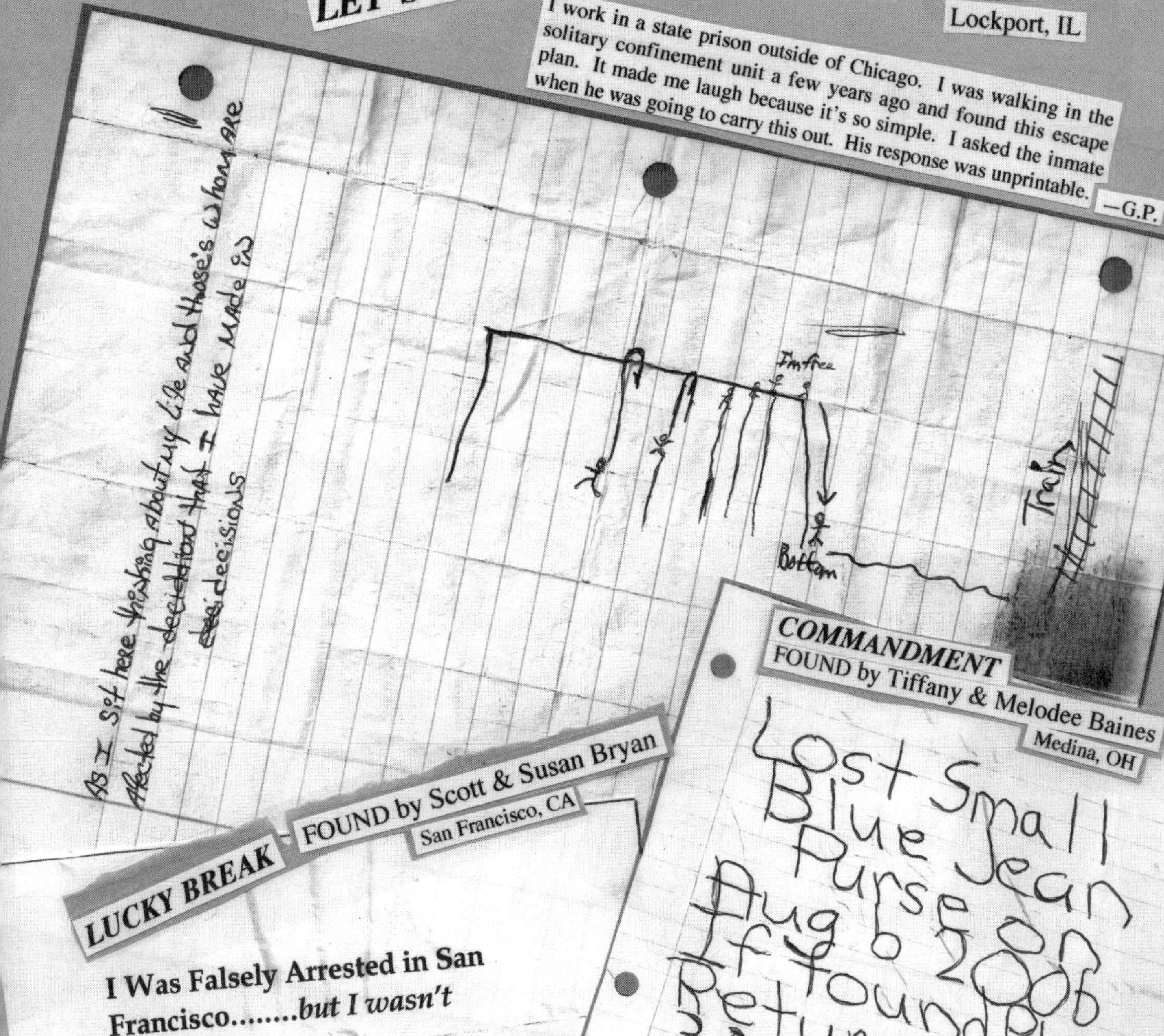

As I sit here thinking about my life and those's whom are affected by the decision that I have made in their decisions

[hand-drawn escape plan diagram with stick figures, labeled "I'm free", "Bottom", and "Train"]

COMMANDMENT
FOUND by Tiffany & Melodee Baines
Medina, OH

Lost Small Blue Jean Purse on Aug o 2006 If found please Return to 431 304 Thou shall Not steal or Take Something that Does Not Belong to you

LUCKY BREAK
FOUND by Scott & Susan Bryan
San Francisco, CA

I Was Falsely Arrested in San Francisco........but I wasn't tortured.

Signed by:

_____

Birth Name

△ Check here if a veteran of U.S. Military Duty

Collection points will be announced shortly.

SHY GIRL SHY GIRL UPDATE!

now wearing nice colors instead of LONG SLEEVED SWEATERS and BLACK PANTS

Lake Calhoun
Spring 2006

1. I smile and wave, rather aggressively. You smile back!

2. Animal instincts inside me make me **chase** you;
"DON'T YOU RECOGNIZE ME?" "I DON'T KNOW WHO YOU ARE."
"OK — BUT DON'T YOU RECOGNIZE ME?" "BUT I DON'T KNOW WHO YOU ARE!!"

3 It takes me about five seconds; I can't **believe** it!
It IS you! "COMON!!" I growl, as in
"Comon, let's do this (Summer 2006)". You do smile.
Smile (thanks) and you keep on walking.
Good for you. "YOU KNOW HOW TO GET IN TOUCH WITH ME!"
I yell, assuming, hoping you've seen a flyer

If we're going to have our SPECTACULAR Summer 2006
love affair, you've got to meet me part-way!
If you already have husbands and boyfriends,
they will just have to concede that I love you more!
I'm gonna keep **running**, and I hope to see you again!

Evan

evxanadu   evstar at gmail

Charming romantic or creepy stalker? What do *you* think of Evan's unusual campaign? Email us [shygirl@foundmagazine.com] and let us know what you think! We'll print some of your responses in our next issue, along with some of our correspondence with the man behind these flyers, and our own take on things. Meanwhile, to learn more about the mystery flyers and see Evan unmasked, go to YouTube, search for 'Shy girl shy girl,' and check out the Fox News investigative report! — DAVY

Birmingham, Alabama
July 27, 1943

PERSONAL AND CONFIDENTIAL

MEMORANDUM FOR SPECIAL AGENT ELMER LINHEART JACOBSEN:

RE: UNKNOWN SUBJECT; Explosion L and N Railroad
    Train #2, Car #1894, Birmingham Division,
    11:15 AM, June 9, 1943 near Oxmoor, Alabama.
    SABOTAGE

Reference is made to your report dated July 26, 1943 in the above entitled matter in which you designated 5 copies for the Bureau and 3 copies for the Birmingham Field Division. If you had taken the trouble to review this file, you would have noted that G-2 Atlanta had been advised of this matter, and you would have also noted that you had indicated a copy for G-2 Atlanta in a previous report. However, in your report of July 26, 1943, you failed to designate this copy, thereby indicating that you had not taken the trouble to thoroughly prepare your dictation and review the file.

I would not have taken this means of bringing this matter to your attention except for the fact that you have indicated a great deal of carelessness in submitting investigative reports recently. On some occasions you have dictated an investigative report on a case and then in about 3 or 4 days, before report had been typed up, you would be ready to dictate another report.

In other instances similar negligence in designating the copies of the reports has been noted, and in connection with some sabotage cases it has been necessary, because of your tendency to be verbose, to make corrections on every single page of your reports.

MEMORANDUM FOR SA JACOBSEN
Page Two
July 27, 1943

PERSONAL AND CONFIDENTIAL

The stenographers have recently advised that you need to prepare better for your dictation. They state that on numerous occasions you will dictate a report and then go to the stenographer on 4 or 5 occasions before it is transcribed to insert additions which you had forgotten to dictate. In one instance you sent one stenographer 4 routing slips containing inserts on one report.

They likewise have stated that you have the mistaken impression that all of your reports are expedite, you do not prepare notes in logical order, have not reviewed the files to ascertain definitely who is origin, what leads remain to be covered, and what the proper status of the report is.

The above matters are brought to your attention in order that you may make some effort to improve your ability in report writing. I feel sure that if you will spend sufficient time in preparing your dictation, and during this time will thoroughly review the file upon which you are to dictate, you can improve your ability to a considerable degree.

(Signed) D. K. BROWN, SAC

25

CONTINUES →

OMAHA P D
22900 8·27·45
24-5-'6-/33

Just a couple of months after being suspended for losing his gun while on duty, Elmer gets reamed by his supervisor for his ineptitude at filing reports.

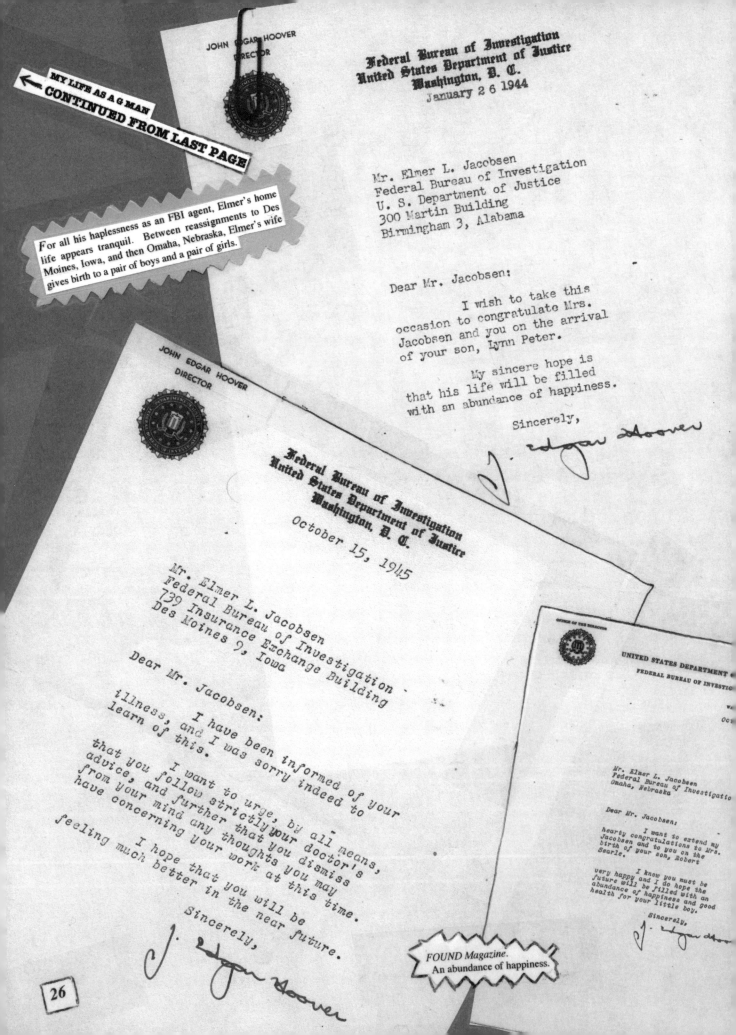

For all his haplessness as an FBI agent, Elmer's home life appears tranquil. Between reassignments to Des Moines, Iowa, and then Omaha, Nebraska, Elmer's wife gives birth to a pair of boys and a pair of girls.

JOHN EDGAR HOOVER
DIRECTOR

Federal Bureau of Investigation
United States Department of Justice
Washington, D. C.
January 2 6 1944

Mr. Elmer L. Jacobsen
Federal Bureau of Investigation
U. S. Department of Justice
300 Martin Building
Birmingham 3, Alabama

Dear Mr. Jacobsen:

I wish to take this occasion to congratulate Mrs. Jacobsen and you on the arrival of your son, Lynn Peter.

My sincere hope is that his life will be filled with an abundance of happiness.

Sincerely,

J. Edgar Hoover

JOHN EDGAR HOOVER
DIRECTOR

Federal Bureau of Investigation
United States Department of Justice
Washington, D. C.
October 15, 1945

Mr. Elmer L. Jacobsen
Federal Bureau of Investigation
739 Insurance Exchange Building
Des Moines 9, Iowa

Dear Mr. Jacobsen:

I have been informed of your illness, and I was sorry indeed to learn of this.

I want to urge, by all means, that you follow strictly your doctor's advice, and further that you dismiss from your mind any thoughts you may have concerning your work at this time.

I hope that you will be feeling much better in the near future.

Sincerely,

J. Edgar Hoover

OFFICE OF THE DIRECTOR

UNITED STATES DEPARTMENT
FEDERAL BUREAU OF INVESTIG

OC

Mr. Elmer L. Jacobsen
Federal Bureau of Investigatio
Omaha, Nebraska

Dear Mr. Jacobsen:

I want to extend my hearty congratulations to Mrs. Jacobsen and to you on the birth of your son, Robert Searle.

I know you must be very happy and I do hope the future will be filled with an abundance of happiness and good health for your little boy.

Sincerely,

J. Edgar Hoover

FOUND Magazine.
An abundance of happiness.

Dear Spaatzie: We are still thinking of you
and hope that you are keeping out of the way of
and naughty children in the neighborhood. I
     know that you miss Toodles as we do too and
     believe me we surely grieve for her — that poor
     little sister of yours — my dear little pet —
No one could have ever made me believe that she
would have been let out long enough to chase cars.
The two of you were naughty when together that is why
I made you stay in the house while I let Toodles go
out; and then only go out after the children went to
school — after nine. I hope you feel more cheerful
you looked so dejected and subdued. I sure want you
with us just as soon as the powers that be can or will
arrange for it.   Fondly your Mistress and Master

15 Sept '48

GREETINGS FROM COUNCIL BLUFFS IOWA

Then trouble strikes again. Elmer and his family have been
house-sitting and dog-sitting in Omaha for a Naval officer
and his wife who are stationed abroad in Iceland. The full
story emerges in a series of postcards from the Naval
officer's wife—some addressed to Elmer, most addressed to
Spaatzie, the surviving cocker spaniel.

'You promised to keep me informed about my dogs—gentleman's agreement. I would like you to refresh my
mind as to where you buried Toodles + the details of her death. How's Spaatzie? A photo of her if you please!'

O.C. KEFLAVIK Air Base
" Iceland

Miss Spaatzie Bisette
1321 'Y' Street
Omaha Nebraska USA

'Dear Spaatzie: We are still in the land of the living. We think of you every day—hope you are keeping well and happy.
We hope to be home one of these days. Winter is setting in there—our mail may be delayed from time to time. The
folks promised to send me you and Toodles' pictures from time to time. I can't remember where they buried Toodles. I
wish they would tell me. Be good doggie. Wag your tail + keep smiling as you really know how for a dog.'

'You promised me you would take care of my pets. Toodles was no dog to roam—she loved the house.
It is hard to believe you would do that to me. I considered your four children hoping you'd appreciate
my home and keep my pets alive. Poor Spaatzie is lonesome. If you had slapped my face and stuck a
dagger in my heart you couldn't have hurt me more. One postcard July 1st from April first!!!'

ISLAND

POST CARD

27

MY LIFE AS A G MAN CONTINUES →

"Sioux Falls, S.D.
March 29, 1952

"I, Kenneth Allen Kitts, make the following voluntary statement to Elmer L. Jacobsen who I know to be a Special Agent of the Federal Bureau of Investigation. No promises, threats, or any other inducements have been made to me for this statement. I know that I do not have to make this statement & that I may consult an attorney concerning it.

"I am 34 years old having been born 4/20/17 at Kansas City, Mo. I am presently residing in the U.S. Penitentiary at Leavenworth, Ka.

"In about 8/50 I became personally associated with Pasquale Joseph Belcastro in Omaha, Nebr. In the summer of 1950 I was called upon by Yancy Douglas Hardy due to a common friend causing our introduction to each other. Hardy was then residing in Tyler, Tex, with his wife & family.

"About Oct. 3 or 4, 1950, Belcastro with his 1950 4 door, two tone grey Nash Ambassador took Hardy & me to Sioux City, Ia, from Omaha. We made this trip preparatory to casing the bank at Garretson, S.D. for burglary. I had been informed several months before that this bank had a lot of money in the safe & in the safety deposit boxes. My source of information was Tony Prochelo who is a friend of _____ Noltze, Sioux City, Ia., Oldsmobile dealer. Tony Prochelo said that Noltze was a part owner of the Garretson Bank. While drinking at Prochelo's Turin Inn Noltze had mentioned an old woman safety deposit box holder who had considerable cash in her box. Noltze was said to have stated that he & Wangsness, the Cashier of the bank, had examined the contents of this box & found it "loaded" with money. I further recall that Tony Prochelo & I went to Garretson, S.D. in about June, 1950, to look the bank over from outside.

Fresh Woes Confront Kitts

Now Charged With S.D. Bank Robbery

Kenneth Kitts, to whom arrest is an annoyance and bail bond a business expense, faced new annoyances and expenses Wednesday.

The well-dressed 33-year-old Omaha burglar was arrested about 7:40 p. m. Wednesday at the Last Chance Cafe, a tavern at 3760 West Broadway, Council Bluffs—less than seven hours after he had been arrested at his home, 3313 Turner Boulevard, Omaha.

The Council Bluffs arrest was made by Federal Bureau of Investigation agents on a complaint filed Wednesday in Sioux Falls, S. D.

Cashier Slugged

It charges Kitts with participation in a kidnaping and $2,991 robbery at the First National Bank of Garretson, S. D., last October 4.

The local FBI office said that three men went to the home of Tom Wangsness, cashier of the bank, and forced him to give them keys to the bank and the combination of the vault. Mr. Wangsness was slugged with a gun.

Kitts, as natty as a man can be after a night in jail, appeared before United States Commissioner Addison C. Kistle in Council Bluffs Thursday morning and asked for a preliminary hearing. This was set for 1 p. m. D...

- 2 -

"About the last week in 9/50 I began talking to Leo Prochelo Tony's brother, about the Garretson bank and about what would be the problems of burglarizing it. I had Leo describe to Noltze a "niggerhead" safe & waited while Noltze was shown one by Leo Prochelo. Leo quoted Noltze as saying that the Garretson safe inside the vault was a square affair & much like the one Noltze had in his office. Leo also quoted Noltze as saying that the Garretson safe had about $200,000 in it. I did not want Noltze to see me & therefore I did all my dealing with Noltze through Leo Prochelo. Leo established from Noltze that Wangsness lived in a white home on the opposite side of the bank but on the opposite corner 3 or 4 blocks south of the same street as the bank.

"The afternoon Belcastro, Hardy & I went to Sioux City, Ia., I left the car at the Turin Inn where I remained while Hardy & Belcastro went on to Garretson to familiarize themselves with the residence of Cashier Wangsness.

"I was still at the Turin Inn with Leo Prochelo when Hardy & Belcastro, at 700p, returned to the Turin Inn. They advised that they had been unable to locate the Cashiers house & mentioned that his was not listed in the phone. Then I had Leo Prochelo call Noltze & report the above negative information. Noltze was quoted by Prochelo as saying that Wangsness did live in a Garretson white house with picture window in front.

"Then Hardy, Belcastro, and I ate at the table of Ray Friedman, Sioux City produce Co. operator. I believe his blonde wife was also at the table. About 830P, 10/3/50 we set out for Garretson in Belcastro's car. We went there on U. S. Hwy. 75 in Ia. until we turned west towards Garretson. We probably arrived Garretson about 11 P.M.

"To locate the Wangsness residence Hardy made inquiry of a lady in a corner house & was told that Wangsness lived diagonally across the street. We noted that the Wangsness house was dark. While discussing what to do about this apparent absence, we observed a 4 door light blue Buick car drive up to the Wangsness garage. A man & woman got out of the car & entered the house.

We would have stopped these people from entering the house if another car had not driven up at the time and the occupants have conversation with the first arrivals.

"When the lights went out in the Wangsness house we drove out of town temporarily & then, upon our return we entered the house through a side-rear door. As we entered I cut the telephone wire near this door. We were all wearing brown army coveralls which I had just bought in a Sioux City Army-Navy Store near a viaduct on the east end of downtown Sioux City. Hardy & Belcastro put on silk stocking caps to later use as masks when pulled down over the face.

"After we entered the house, I remained downstairs while Hardy & Belcastro in stocking feet went upstairs to take the people in custody. After I heard conversation upstairs, I knew the people were in custody. I then walked upstairs & told Hardy & Belcastro to have the people turn face down in bed so they could not see me. I was not wearing any mask.

"I carried on the conversation with the man in bed who said he was Wangsness & claimed he had just got back from a party in Sioux Falls. I noted that blood was running from Wangsness' head onto the sheet on the right side of the bed as I faced it. I told Hardy who was on that side of the bed that he should not have hit Wangsness.

"I secured the keys to the bank from Wangsness pants pocket & the combination to the vault from him. Hardy & Belcastro tied up the Wangsness' with wire.

"Then Belcastro & I went to the bank alone while Hardy guarded Mr. & Mrs. Wangsness. I could not open the vault so Belcastro & I went back to the Wangsness house & untied Mr. Wangsness. I drove his Buick down to the bank with him blindfolded between me & Belcastro. We had left Belcastro's Nash 1 block east of the Wangsness house.

"Back at the bank with Wangsness' car parked out in front, I had Wangsness open the vault. I shut the burglar alarm off in the vault & left Belcastro to guard Wangsness in the front of the bank while serving as a lookout.

- 3 -

"About the safe in the vault, Wangsness said it contained $11,000 cash but had a time lock which would not permit opening until 10°° A.M. He told me where the bank's money was in the vault. I found it & put it in cloth money bags. It had been in drawers. Then in my hurry to get out of the bank I left a bag of currency behind. It contained between $2,000 and $3,000. Everything else was various denominations of silver.

"Belcastro & I then took Wangsness back to his house & tied him up again in bed probably leaving his clothes on. Then we went to Belcastro's Nash & headed east to U.S. Hwy, 75 where we turned south to Sioux City & visited the Turin Inn. Leo Prochelo was still waiting for us though it was daylight, probably 5 A.M. We would have been there earlier if we hadn't returned 15 miles or further to Garretson to pick up the bag of currency. We did not go to the bank for it because we saw the lights on in the Wangsness house.

"I told Leo Prochelo about forgetting the currency but that we had secured about $3,000. I offered him 10% for his assistance but he did not want it because we had not been able to get in the safe & therefore had not made much of a score.

"I think I got rid of all the silver to Donald James Paltani, Omaha car dealer. I gave him something for handling this silver--probably $100 to $150. I made this delivery in South Omaha, Nebr.

"I have read the above statement consisting of this and 5 other ink-written pages. I find it to be true. No promises threats or inducements have been made to me for this statements.

"I have initialed each page, correction, and addition.

Witnessed;

Elmer L. Jacobsen, SA., F.B.I., Omaha.
John W. Gallagher Deputy U.S. Marshal, Dist. of Ka...

/s/ Kenneth Allen Kitts

Kitts, who likes to present the appearance of a young business man with plenty of double-breasted suits, simple, high-priced jewelry, had been arrested at 1 p. m. Wednesday on a warrant charging participation in the burglary, November 3 of the Laurens (Ia.) State Bank, in which $38,246

- 4 -

Bank Robber Flees From Prison Guards

OMAHA, Sept. 14 (UP)—Kenneth Kitts, convicted bank robber and escape artist, broke away from guards here today at the Douglas county courthouse and fled.

Police surrounded the courthouse and threw tear gas bombs in the basement.

One report said Kitts was seen driving away in an auto with two other men.

BUT AUTHORITIES and police believed he might be hiding in the basement.

Kitts, serving a long prison term as an habitual criminal, was brought here from the Nebraska state penitentiary at Lincoln to testify in a federal hearing.

Police said he eluded penitentiary guards this afternoon about 4 p.m. He was wearing prison denims.

Warden Herbert Hann was among the group who escorted Kitts here.

HE HAD TESTIFIED in the hearing about his part in a $100,000 jewel robbery at Oklahoma City in May, 1949. He said he slugged a jeweler after trailing him for four days and stole a suitcase full of diamonds.

Kitts escaped from Linn county jail at Cedar Rapids, Ia., while being held for robbery of the Laurens, Ia., state bank. He was captured, convicted and taken to Lincoln to serve an earlier term first. While there, he confessed the jewelry robbery.

But even Elmer's triumphs have a way of fizzling. Kenneth Kitts escapes from jail just a few months after his arrest. He's apprehended quickly, but then escapes again, this time, seemingly, for good.

MY LIFE AS A G MAN CONTINUES ON PAGE 50

Name _Tom Shea_

Date _3-30-06_   **Period** _666_ ⊕

ALTERNATIVES TO DRINKING

Lonely, Sad, Depressed

If a person feels lonely, sad, or depressed, instead of drinking he or she can:

1. Lament over personal failure.

2. Realize nothing means anything.

3. Hang it up.

Angry

If a person feels angry, instead of drinking he or she can:

1. Plot a smear campaign.

2. Hurt oneself, physically.

3. Take out frustrations on elderly OR homeless.

Insecure, Shy, Nervous

If a person feels shy, insecure, or nervous, instead of drinking he or she can:

1. Practice keeping comments/ opinions to self.

2. Stay indoors.

3. Feign Confidence.

Bored

If a person feels bored, instead of drinking he or she can:

1. Ignore someone.

2. Order pizza to neighbor's house. Watch confusion/anger ensue from window. Repeat.

3. Fuck Something.

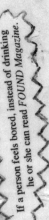

If a person feels bored, instead of drinking he or she can read FOUND Magazine.

30

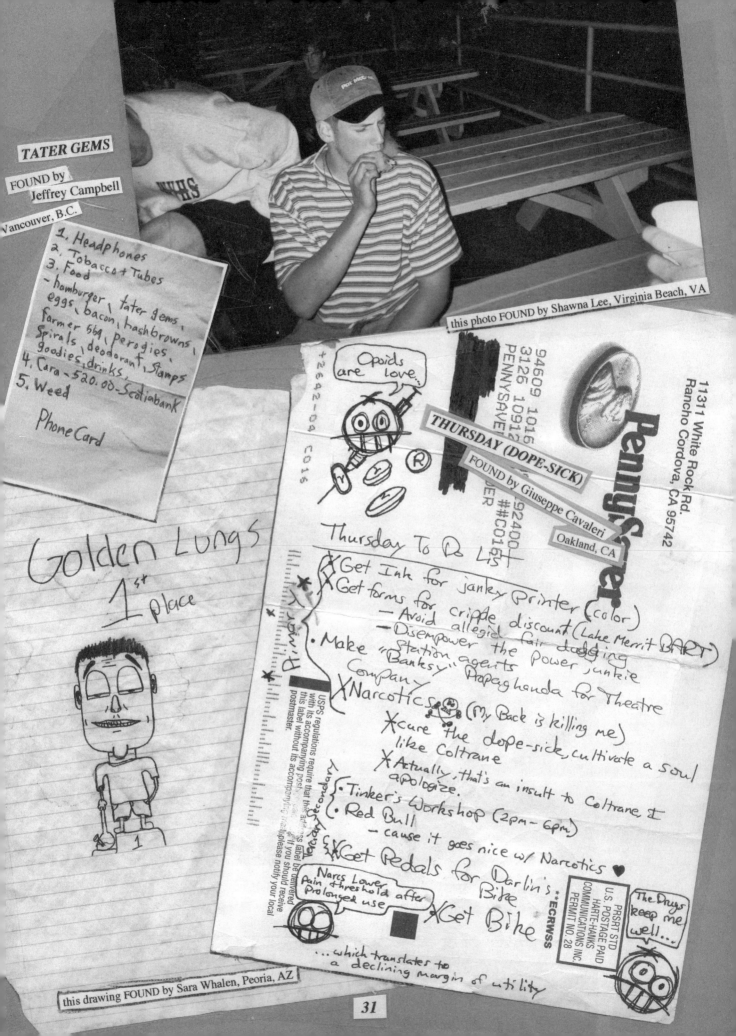

TATER GEMS

FOUND by
Jeffrey Campbell

Vancouver, B.C.

1. Headphones
2. Tobacco + Tubes
3. Food
   - hamburger, tater gems,
   eggs, bacon, hashbrowns,
   farmer sog, perogies,
   spirals, deodorant, stamps
   goodies, drinks,
4. Cara - $20.00 - Scotiabank
5. Weed

Phone Card

this photo FOUND by Shawna Lee, Virginia Beach, VA

Golden Lungs
1st place

1

this drawing FOUND by Sara Whalen, Peoria, AZ

11311 White Rock Rd.
Rancho Cordova, CA 95742

PennySaver

94609 1016
3126 10912
PENNYSAVER
#C016

THURSDAY (DOPE-SICK)
FOUND by Giuseppe Cavaleri
Oakland, CA

Opoids
are love...

Thursday To Do List
X Get Ink for janky Printer (color)
X Get forms for cripple discount (Lake Merrit BART)
   - Avoid allegied fair dodging
   - Disempower the Power junkie
   station agents
• Make "Banksy" Propaghanda for Theatre
   Company
X Narcotics (My Back is killing me)
   X cure the dope-sick, cultivate a soul
   like Coltrane
   X Actually, that's an insult to Coltrane I
   apologize.
• Tinker's Workshop (2pm - 6pm)
• Red Bull
   - cause it goes nice w/ Narcotics ♥
X Get Pedals for Darlin's Bike
   X Get Bike

Narcs Lower
Pain threshold after
Prolonged use

...which translates to
a declining margin of utility

The Drugs
keep me
well...

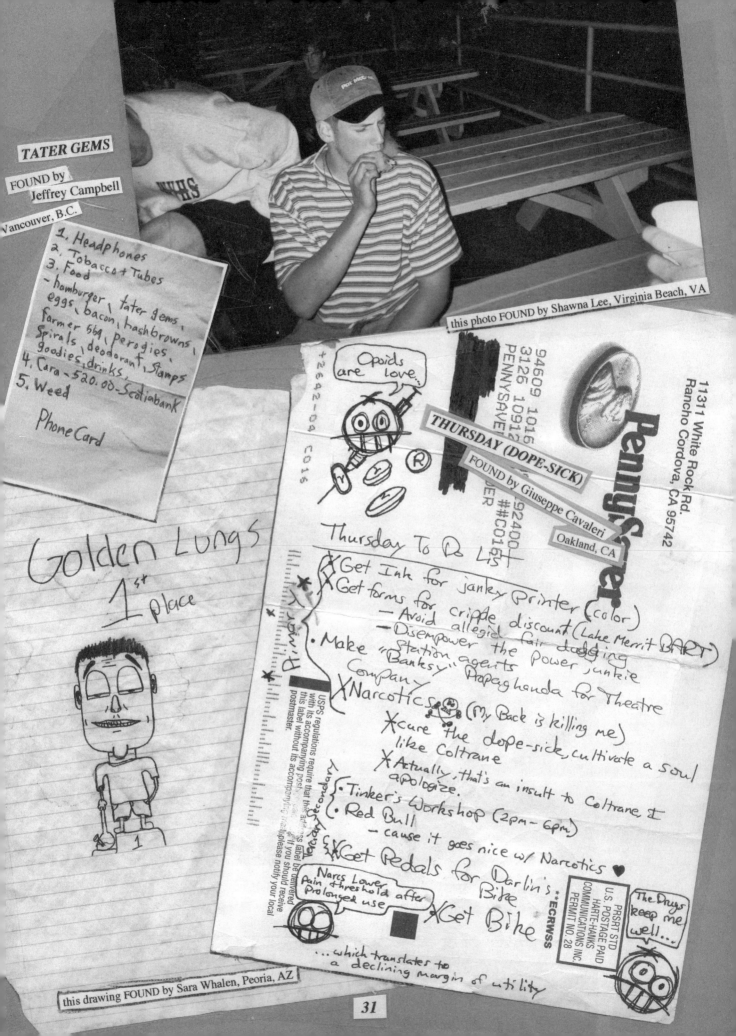

USPS regulations require that the address label
with its accompanying postage
this label without its accompanying post.
postmaster.

Priority

please notify your local
accompanying mailplease receive
accompanying mail, be delivered
if you should receive
Priority Access

**ECRWSS

PRSRT STD
U.S. POSTAGE PAID
HARTE-HANKS
COMMUNICATIONS INC.
PERMIT NO. 28

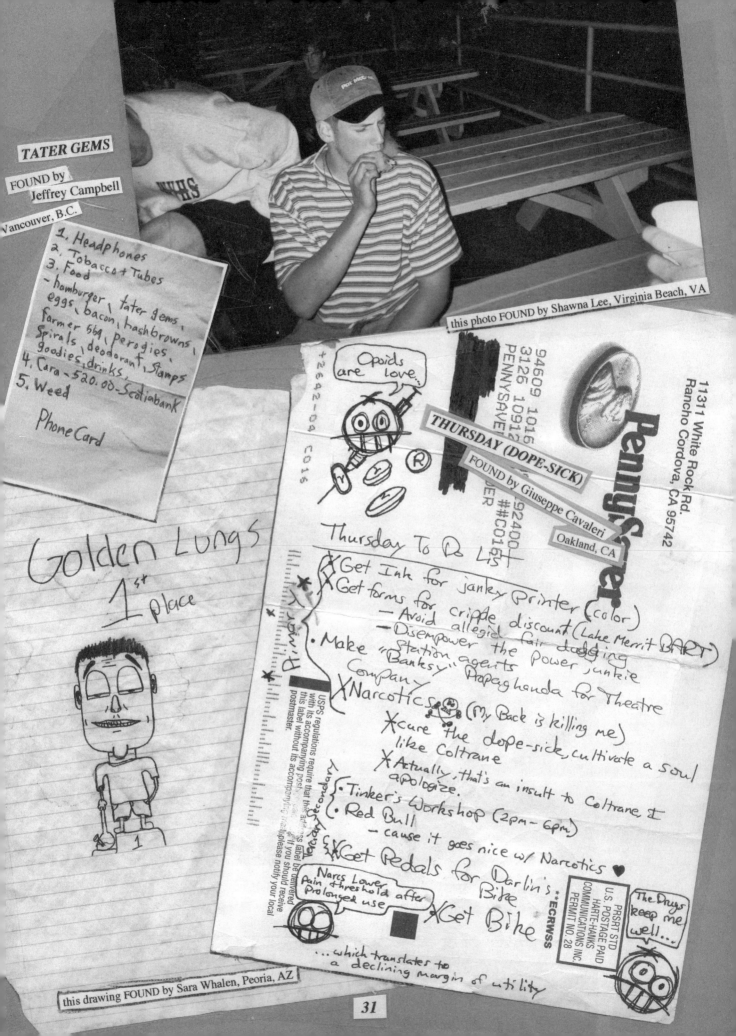

Trisha M.

THE BADDEST NISSANS IN THE NORTHWEST

FOUND by Devon Driscoll

Oregon City, OR

This letter had never been opened, so Trisha M. has never read this letter. I found it in a flowerbed in front of a church, framed with dirt chunks. I wonder if perhaps it fell out of J.J.'s pocket and was placed there by a stranger, hoping the owner would find it again. It's the most amazing and heartbreaking thing I've ever found.

—D.D.

illustrations by Sarah Locke

I remember...

It must have been around October, because it was cold and wet, a friend of mine and I decided to go grab a cup of coffee at the bottom of the hill, for lack of anything better to do. After being seated we started to B.S. about something or another when I saw you, your hair was pulled back in a beautiful french braid running down your back, and your greeting was as warm as the coffee you were pouring into my cup. That was the first time I had ever saw you, and it was all I needed.

Usually, for a guy like me, it would have been impossible to let an intelligent word come out of my mouth, but you seemed to be so easy to talk to. In the weeks/months to follow, you befriended me, a scraggly, creepy looking (at the time) boy who had no clue as to who he was or where he was headed in life. I was amazed at the fact that you didn't give a shit about the morbid garb or the demeanor I had used to pretty much fend off most everybody with. After I had gotten to know you well enough, I started trying my best to find the right words and the perfect time to ask you out, but at the time my lack of self-confidence and fear of rejection wouldn't allow the words to escape from me. We became friends, and started hanging out frequently, and I realized how much of a warm, open-minded, sure footed person you were. At a time when I had made a poor decision to get involved with a very bad disease called drug abuse,

→

33

I found it harder and harder to find ways to talk to you about how I felt. The shit really started to fuck me up pretty bad and for awhile all I could think of, it was to go and see you at work, drinking cup after cup trying for the life of me to figure out how I would tell you how I felt.

I know I probably seemed like some kind of psycho or something, but I was so f***ed up. After countless, sleepless nights, hanging out with a bunch of cracked out morons, wanting nothing more than to kill the pain of coming down just so I could think about the one beautiful thing in my life, I went a little crazy. I'm sure there were times when you thought to yourself, "what's up with that crazy bastard." All I was trying to do was put myself in a place where I could forget about how much of an idiot I was for never even trying to open up to you.

Months passed, and I found myself hanging out with a little different crowd trying to convince myself that there was no possible way you could ever feel the same way about me as I did for you.

During that time, in an attempt to let go, I met another girl whom I thought might just be my reason for getting you out of my head.

FOUND Magazine. WRITE US! 3455 charing cross • ann arbor, mi • 48108 E-MAIL US! info @ foundmagazine.com

Again, the drugs still had control of my life, and as I persued her for months, I felt as if I was doomed to be alone for ~~the~~ rest of my life.

Even though I thought I had finally found someone to fill the empty hole in my heart, she didn't seem to want anything to do with me. After awhile, one of my friends convinced me that nothing would ever happen between her and I. On the very day I had decided to walk away from trying to get her to realize that I existed something happened between us, and that started me on my way to the life I have now.

After about a year I started thinking that maybe I had made a bad decision, and that I was too eager to end my lonliness, when I found out she was pregnant with my son. I didn't know what to do, and all the while I still thought of you almost every day. I decided that I had to do the right thing and except my responsibility. Even though prior to the "big surprise", we were on the verge of saying goodbye to one another, I felt I could learn to love her as the mother of my child. I don't regret my decision, for I love my son more than anything in the world, and he has changed my life completly.

#1 DAD

But I still feel a little empty inside,
they say that theres one person in
everyones life that is "The One".
And eight years after that ~~night~~
rainy October night, and that very
special cup of coffee,
I still find myself thinking about you everyday,
I fell in love with you Toisha,
ever since the first day I ever saw you,
and when I think and try to deny it,
I end up running into you, and for the
five or ten fleeting minutes that we talk
about everything and nothing at all,
those are the times when I feel
more alive than ever.
I know that we both have separate lives,
and separate goals and dreams,
and I have a great amount of responsibility
with raising my son with his mother and father
both around to help him prepare for this
seemingly saddening world, I want you
to know that I won't ever
love anyone as much as I love you.
And no matter how long in between
our run-ins with each other,
I'll still think and dream about you all the time.
I don't want you to read this and feel
any kind of pressure to respond, or to think
of me any differently, I'm still your friend
either way, I just couldn't hold it in any longer.

FOUND Magazine. After you read this,
you'll probably look at me alot differently.

I've spent my life holding in feelings
just to do the right thing,
and I just had to let you know how
I feel, and how I will always feel about you
for the rest of my life,
the last time we talked, you told me
that you might end up travelling in the near future,
and that prompted me to find some kind of
way to say these things before it was too late.
I know we both have our own paths to follow,
I've always known that you were born to be
a healer, not only with your learned abilities,
but with your warmth and caring,
and with your presence in general.
It took me a little longer to find myself,
but I realized that I was meant to be
fast, and to race and build the baddest nissans
in the northwest, and I'll get there one day.
But most importantly I'm a father,
and I want to raise my son to be
proud, sensible, caring, and in general, a person
you don't see too often in this world anymore.
One day soon I really want you to see him again.
I know the last time was brief, and he was still
very young, but he is something special, even though
he can be a handful sometimes.
I want you to know that, after you read this,
you'll probably look at me alot differently, you may take
it as you will, but no matter what happens in our lives,
I'll be there for you if you need me, as a friend,
or maybe one day something more. forever yours K.C.

THE PRISON GUARD POET

FOUND by Rachel Miller

On a Fremont-Richmond BART train in California, I found several soulful handwritten poems by W. Joseph Stegner, apparently a former prison guard. This was my favorite. — R.M.

I Have Never Been To Switzerland

I have never been to Switzerland,
to Germany or France. To climb a tree in Windermere
I haven't had the chance.

A monsoon never bathed me
and a rice field wet me not.
I have never watched the sun rise
from a prarie horse's trot.

Never have I kissed the moon
from the mountains of Tibet
or lived within a desert
begging life itself for wet.

I have never watched the Earth spin
from an orbit out in space,
or felt the wounds of battle
ripping bullets in my face.

I have never screamed in terror
as the bombs fell from the sky
and I have never watched an army
make my living loved ones die.

But I've been a paramedic
on the lands where greats have walked
with the richest of the rich
and the poorest poor I've talked.

I've loved the dead and dying
with the passion of my life
and held a mother crying
from the news of her worst strife.

The civil war that we rename
that shares the same hate's end
has found that my employment
did to all camps neutral send.

When the East side shot the West side
and believed that lives were just
or the red cloth stabbed the blue cloth
with a steel blade in the bust,

I loved both sides and listened well
to the reasons of their hate —
and behold misinformation
was the breader of such fate.

When one side thought the other
was just less then something whole,
yet the time to understand someone
saturated not the soul.

When assumptions have more value
than the wisdom of the greats,
and excuses are imagined
to excuse our living hates...

When we think that morals give us right
to lessen someone's worth,
dis-eases become justified
by the arrogant on earth.

Life is always sacred
by the fact that we exist
and deception is the ruler
of why people clench their fist.

Joseph Stegner
9-16-00

All of us share life itself
and that makes us all kin,
when we see not our equality
we are blind somewhere within.

We were shown to love our enemies
because love is what
but the lists of our best
causes all the world's exclusions
unrest.

Hatred is a plague
that is a curse
it assumes superiority upon the Earth,
to denounce another's worth.

If we do not love all people
who are living in our view,
how can we see what is really know,
if what is best is what we do?

Love's the only lamp in dead
for it alone can listen well —
all other forms of feeling
produce assumption's toxil smell.

It is time for Evolution
on the surface of the Earth —
which begins by choice within us
to acknowledge other's worth.

Equality is a truth.
W. Joseph Stegner
9-16-00

Equality is mentioned
by the service of our lips
but our actions prove that otherwise
is wherefrom our heart sips.

The Golden Rule is golden
by the equal that it knows
and treats all souls accordingly
whereer its law goes.

But instead we place our values
by the titles that we make
and legalize the reasons
to another's freedom take.

People do for money
what they do not understand
and believe they're told so
they can bring ill on the land.

I saw this when I was a guard
at a ranch paid by the state
to assume the world was bettered
by a razor-wire fate.

Inmates were called criminals
and known by number's length
who they truly were inside
was masked by label's strength.

As a medic and a prison guard
and all the other hats I wore
I've learned that inside everyone
there is a spot we should adore

SHERIFF
OMAHA
10 24 52
4333

Joseph Stegner
9-16-00

I usually think it's kinda wack when magazines print letters from readers praising their magazine—it's just got a self-congratulatory air about it. However, there's something about the letters we receive from prisoners requesting copies of the magazine (in accordance with our policy to send free mags to inmates) that is *so* sweet and rich, I've backed down from my harsh "no-letters-to-FOUND" stance and decided to share some of them with you here over the next several pages, along with a couple of finds sent in by FOUND readers in prison. To those behind bars: keep your head up. The FOUND family is thinking about you and has got your back.
— DAVY

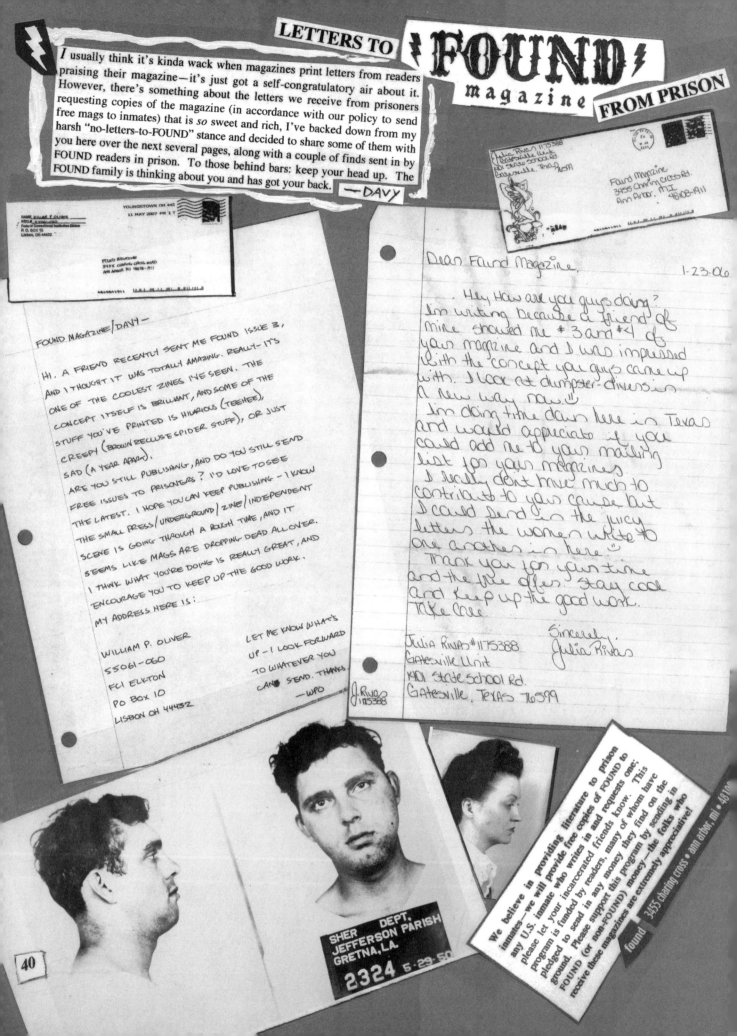

FOUND MAGAZINE/DAVY—

HI. A FRIEND RECENTLY SENT ME FOUND ISSUE 3, AND I THOUGHT IT WAS TOTALLY AMAZING. REALLY- ITS ONE OF THE COOLEST ZINES I'VE SEEN. THE CONCEPT ITSELF IS BRILLIANT, AND SOME OF THE STUFF YOU'VE PRINTED IS HILARIOUS (TEEHEE) OR JUST CREEPY (BROWN RECLUSE SPIDER STUFF), OR JUST SAD (A YEAR APART).

ARE YOU STILL PUBLISING, AND DO YOU STILL SEND FREE ISSUES TO PRISONERS? I'D LOVE TO SEE THE LATEST. I HOPE YOU CAN KEEP PUBLISHING — I KNOW THE SMALL PRESS/UNDERGROUND/ZINE/INDEPENDENT SCENE IS GOING THROUGH A ROUGH TIME, AND IT SEEMS LIKE MAGS ARE DROPPING DEAD ALL OVER. I THINK WHAT YOU'RE DOING IS REALLY GREAT, AND ENCOURAGE YOU TO KEEP UP THE GOOD WORK.

MY ADDRESS HERE IS:

WILLIAM P. OLIVER
55061-060
FCI ELKTON
PO BOX 10
LISBON OH 44432

LET ME KNOW WHAT'S UP — I LOOK FORWARD TO WHATEVER YOU CAN SEND. THANKS.
— WPO

Dear Found Magazine,   1-23-06

Hey, How are you guys doing? Im writing because a friend of mine showed me #3 and #4 of your magzine and I was impressed with the concept you guys came up with. I look at dumpster-diversion a new way now.!!
Im doing time down here in Texas and would appreciate if you could add me to your mailing list for your magzines. I really don't have much to contribute to your cause but I could send in the juicy letters the women write to one another in here.!!
Thank you for your time and the free offer. Stay cool and keep up the good work.
Take Care
                        Sincerely,
                        Julia Rivas

Julia Rivas #1175388
Gatesville Unit
1401 State School Rd.
Gatesville, Texas 76599

SHER DEPT.
JEFFERSON PARISH
GRETNA, LA.
2324   5-29-50

40

Dear FOUND,   12-18-06

Even though my first confirmed find was a turd inside of an old-school, metal STAR WARS lunch box, in an abandoned garage; I'll never forget my first REAL find, a five dollar bill. The out-of-placeness of it just lying there in the lush green grass was a beautiful sight. It blew my young mind. Nothing I have found since has come close to producing the euphoric feeling associated with that early find, and I have found some interesting shit (besides the one in the lunchbox). Like a garbage bag full of weed under a bridge in Decatur, Ill. (it was bunk though), and a quarter-ounce of crack cocaine in the front seat of a car at the junk yard (it was good!), a wallet washed up on the beach by the Santa Monica Pier with $80 in it, a porno mag half buried in the sand on Venice Beach (it was really good 👍), a black kitten meowing in the middle of an Arizona desert. It looked like a buzzard tried to pick his brains out (he made a cool pet), a box of china in an abandoned house, $40 worth of postage stamps in a plastic baggie at the bottom of a flight of stairs, a leather Detroit Pistons ball cap in someones trash (it was way too nice to have been thrown away), $7 on the boardwalk in Santa Monica (only seconds after giving a bag-lady my last 60 cents), and I even found $15,700 in an old purse stashed in my friend's girlfriend's closet. It was really $16,100 but I stuffed $400 in my sock (initial finders fee), then he and I split the rest of it and went to Cali for a few weeks. (It's his ex-girlfriend now.)

But this week, I found FOUND for the first time ever and my paradime has shifted. All of my past "ground scores" now seem very insignificant compared to the amazing scores that grace the pages of FOUND #4. The way I see it, figuring in the street value, I owe FOUND a little over $20,000, but unfortunately I don't have it. I do pledge, from this moment on, to send any found currency to FOUND for the remainder of my life. To reimburse the 20 grand I owe, I am offering a found item of equivalent worth. I originally found it written on the inside of a book while browsing in the library. I showed it to my guy Nate, but due to my un-FOUND consciousness, I left it on the shelf. When your magazine finally awakened my new-FOUND consciousness, I told Nate how I wished I had that script we found at the library so I could bless FOUND with it. Low and behold, Nate had cuffed the book on the sole purpose of it's inner script alone (because

CONTINUED ➡

he thought it was creepy) and had it available in his own personal collection. So without further ado, we bestow upon FOUND "a nice guy like me."

I once was lost, but now I'm FOUND,

Robert E. McKown
P.O. Box 5000
Pekin, Illinois
61555

P.S. Please send me the next issue of FOUND and I promise when I can, I'll order the back issue subscription and your book. Word is bond.

P.S.S. If anybody out there finds my daughter Callista Fern Wright some-where in Arkansas D.O.B 12-13-99 SS# 334-96-8353 please let me know!! She deserves to know that she has a real dad who loves her more than life itself. ☮

Dear Jason & Co:

Thank you for sending an issue

To: FOUND MAGAZINE
3455 Charing Cross Road
Ann Arbor MI 48108

To Whom it Concerns:
I am in the Bard Writing Group at Beacon Correctional Facility in Beacon, New York. Nina, one of the girls who leads the group, brought in clippings from your magazine which we used for a writing assignment. I thought the magazine was a neat concept and Nina said I could request copies. I would like to have sent to me the 4 most recent issues if possible. Your magazine is very cool and I truly enjoyed the writing assignment that came from it.
Thank you
Jeannie Shepler

Send to: Jeannie Shepler # 06g0979
Beacon Correctional Facility
P.O. Box 780
50 Camp Beacon Road
Beacon NY 12508-0780

11/02/06

DAVEY @
FOUND MAGAZINE.
3455 CHARING CROSS. Rd.
ANN HARBOR, MI. 48108-1911

YO DAVEY DUDE,

MAN YOUR MAG KICKS ASS, I'VE BEEN thinkin for YEARS of STARTING SOMETHING up JUST like IT — NEVER DID - THEN BAM I "FOUND" YOUR MAG AND MY IDEA IS REFRESHED ... THANKS - But YO, CHECK THIS - I KNOW YOUR MAG COST $ AND ALL - SO I'M SENDING A STAMPED ENVELOPE to help with SHIPPING COST ... SEE I'M BROKE & LOCKED the fuck up - BUT YOU SAID YOU'D GIVE A FREE COPY OUTS to INMATES - ONLY ONE QUESTION ... MY HOME BOY GOT like A 2002 ISSUE #2 ??! YOU THINK MAYBE I COULD GET ONE OF THE NEWER ISSUES - I'D like to SEE WHAT Y'ALL BEEN DOING NOW - NOT 2 YEARS AGO - ANYWAY - I HOPE to FIND SOME SHIT to SEND you - I GOT A PRETTY BIG COLLECTION OF WEIRD SHIT ALREADY - MAYBE I'LL SHINE! TILL NEXT TIME - "JAG-OFF"

PEACE
VINNY DE
MCC INSRU
POB 777
MONROE, V

Dear Found Magazine:

My name is David Edwards and I am a heavy reader residing at Jessup Pre-Release Unit and my inmate

SOUTHERN MD 207
03 FEB 2008 PM 4 T

PRISON
REQUEST

THE PHOTOGRAPHS

50¢
3/$1.00

You know. I sometime wonder what a nice guy like me is doing in a place like this.. Well maybe I am not as nice as like to think I am. I guess its true, if you ask some of the people of my past they might say I was kinda rotten, selfish, or even down right mean at time. Greedy, sure arn't we all. I can say that I only got mean at people that got in my way. But that would not be true. I was mean when someone started to mass with money that I thougnt I should have. I was mean when someone messed with my drug money. When someone messed with my drugs. See when I had drug I feel good, looked real bad, but felt good. When I had money I thougnt I was a big shot, A sombody. Now I am Just anoter asshole in prison. When people on the street think of me, they say he was a ass. he hit girls and kids he store from everyone who care about him. And you know, some times I wonder what a nice guy like me doing in a place like this with all these bad people.

LAPORE, LOUIE
27;5-6½;118;hr.bk;ey
bn;cp.m dk;bd.md.

43

DEAR FOUND MAGAZINE,

My FRIEND BRYCE RICH of
COVER D'ALAENE IDAHO, WROTE ME &
TOLD ME TO GET A HOLD OF YOU
GUYS. I WAS TOLD YOU SEND FREE
MAGAZINES TO INMATES? I AM
CURRENTLY HOUSED @ SOUTH IDAHO Correctional
I would like to

---

just recently received a letter from a friend
in Portland Oregon, who informed me that you send
magazines free to Prisoners? If this is in fact
true, could in ... ...

To Whom It May Concern: 7-6-04

    I am writing your
magazine company to ask about
getting issues of your magazine.
I am incarcerated in Belmont
Correctional Institution and I
have a friend who is not
incarcerated and gets issues of
your magazine. He said that in

MARIO CARLIN
Booking # 8168451
441 Bauchet St
LOS ANGELES CA 90012   Oct, 12,

hello:
   my name is mario CARLIN I'm curently
INCARCERATED A LOS ANGELES COUNTY JAIL & IM
INTRESTED IN YOUR MAGAZINE Can you Please
SEND me copys of FOUND MAGAZINE
                    THANK YOU.
                    Mario Carlin

4/2/05 SAT 9:45

To:
Someone with a Heart

Today I had the pleasure to look Thru one of your
FOUND magazine. It was enjoyable -n- likable. Today
I'm enclosing a book of stamps value at $7.40. I
would like to have a copy of my own. I'm currently

3-8-04

Davey
      Hey! FIRST OFF I HOPE THIS LETTER REACHES
YOU BECAUSE IM NOT ACTUALLY SURE IF THIS IS IN FACT YOUR
ADDRESS. IM JUST TRYING TO REMEMBER IT FROM READING THE
ISSUE OF FOUND MAGAZINE I BOUGHT PRIOR TO GETTING ARRESTED.

12-31-4

Found.
      I've been hearing about your Publication
for awhile now. I've been trying to wait until
I had some cash to send, but cash is something
that doesn't seem to come in "extras" here. I cant

August 26, 2004

Dear Found Magazine,

      I understand that you have free
subscriptions to people that are incarcerated. Please let me know if thi ...
                    I would like a ...

---

18 May 07 (P.S. Today

Davey,
      Love your magazine "Found",
and nothing could be truer of
people's life. My father use to tell
me "One man's trash is another man's
treasure". Please put me on your
mailing list, and I will contribute
in anyway. Thanks and keep up
the work.
                    Nathan A. Wilson

Address:
Nathan A. Wilson #350354
CWCC-6A-13T
P.O. Box 500
Mitchells, VA 22729

Dear FOUND,

      What up, my name is Ross Pawlak, a local
of ANN ARBOR, currently rotting in the livingston
county Jail. Sucks huh, tell me about it, nothing
better than a bunch of dudes, stinking
like ass and feet, bitching about Jail.
So naturally, me sitting here, I thought about
your help a brotha out with some dope
reading material fund, so help a brotha out!
I think your magazine is tits, I support
the local artist scene in A2, send me some
reading material please, I'm getting sick of
READERS Digest

Sent #3
7/9/...

Missing women,

Ross P - Beotch!

10-1-04

Dear Found Magazine,

      I was informed about your magazine and would truly
Through a good friend of mine and would
appreciate being put on your mailing list.

                    Sincerely,
                    Tim Fleming

Dear Found Magazine,
5-25-07

My name is James Kirby, I'm currintly an inmate in the great ~~shit~~ state of Idaho, they ~~[crossed out]~~ have offered to give me free room and bored for the next several years.

A few weeks ago someone passed me a ragged copy of the third issue of your magazine. It was taped togeather and falling apart but amazingly it seams to be all there and read able. I've never heard of your magazine before but I love it! It was ~~[crossed out]~~ one of the most interesting reads I've had in here. I was exited to see that you provide free copies to inmates, I think that is very kind of you and everyone who supports the programam I realy hope you still do this. As a matter of fact I realy hope your still in publication since the magazine i was given was so old and I've never heard of you before. If so I would realy apreaciate it if you would ~~[crossed out]~~ include

me in your mailing list. It would be great if I could get several issues since I want to read it all I would realy like to get them all (exept the thirc issue since I allready hade that) but if you cant send more than one I would love to get ahold of whatever you can send me. After I get done with them I'll pass them on so other people can enjoy your magazines as much as I did. Thank you so very very much! Please let me know if you cant help me so I'll know not to keep waiting.
My Address is

James Kirby # 67405
ICC/B-204-A
P.O. Box 70010
Boise, ID. 83707

Sincerly,
-Kirby-

Found magazine:

Hey, I found $10 on the ground recently, and thought I'd send it your way.

I like the idea of using found $$ to send the mag to prisoners. So I want $5 of the $10 to go to that program.

I want you to KEEP the other $5 just so you keep doing the magazine and the tours. (You recently came through our town on tour, and I really appreciated that.) Keep up the good work.

-Anonymous

Enormous thanks to everyone who has contributed to our FOUND-to-prisons program!! Your generous donations have allowed us to continue to send magazines to inmates who request them. Each copy of FOUND gets passed around to dozens upon dozens of readers behind bars, so even a small contribution makes a huge difference in many people's lives! Please send in any money you find on the ground (of course, non-FOUND donations are welcome as well). Thanks again—we really appreciate your kindness, and the folks who read the magazines in prison—like James Kirby in Boise, Idaho—are *extremely* grateful.

FOUND ATTN: PRISON FUND
3455 charing cross • ann arbor, mi • 48108

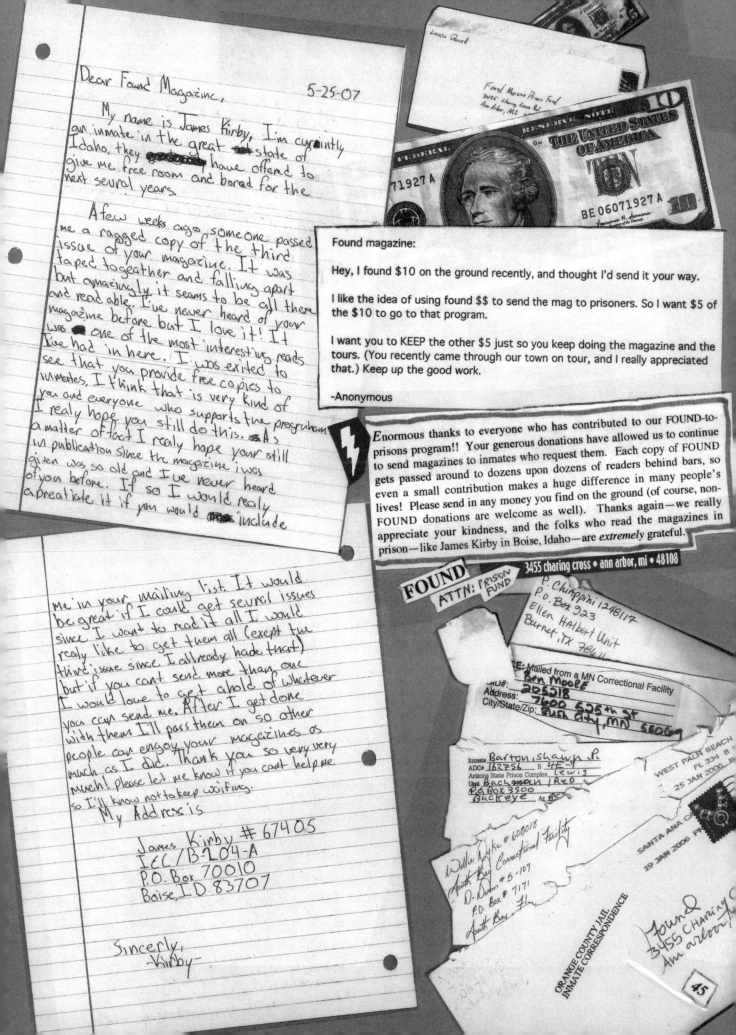

45

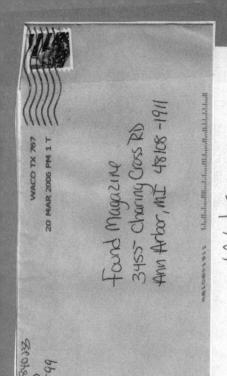

Found Magazine
3455 Charing Cross RD
Ann Arbor, MI 48108-1911

Cynthia Tocin 840132
1401 State School RD
Gatesville TX 76599
Gatesville Unit

Dear Found,   3/19/06

my unit is on lockdown for a semi-annual search. I found this kite Among some stuff. If you print it please send me a copy of the issue. I've seen #'s 3 & 4 and love them. I would Also appreciate anything else you send. Thank you very much!

Peace,
Cynthia

WHAT I HAD TO TELL YOU

FOUND by Cynthia Tucker

Gatesville, TX

can you speed this up please. I'm fighting to stay ~~awake~~ awake 2 1/2 hours of waiting is a bit much.

OKay at first I didnt see you but as a cool friend wanting to be their but now things change cause your not a ugly unbuilt girl at all so what I am saying is now I could see us together, smile. Sorry it took so long, but I was just thinking on how to put things. but this is what I thought about one time.

46

FRONT

it just came to my head when I was falling asleep the day I called you all those ~~name~~ here it goes I just started picturing you. ~~yeah~~ picturing you and your ~~ber~~ breast came to me, ~~yea ndnt dnge~~ and I was Just thinking how it would be to crest on then and Kiss them nibble on them I dont do that alot. but that is it what I had to tell you!

BACK

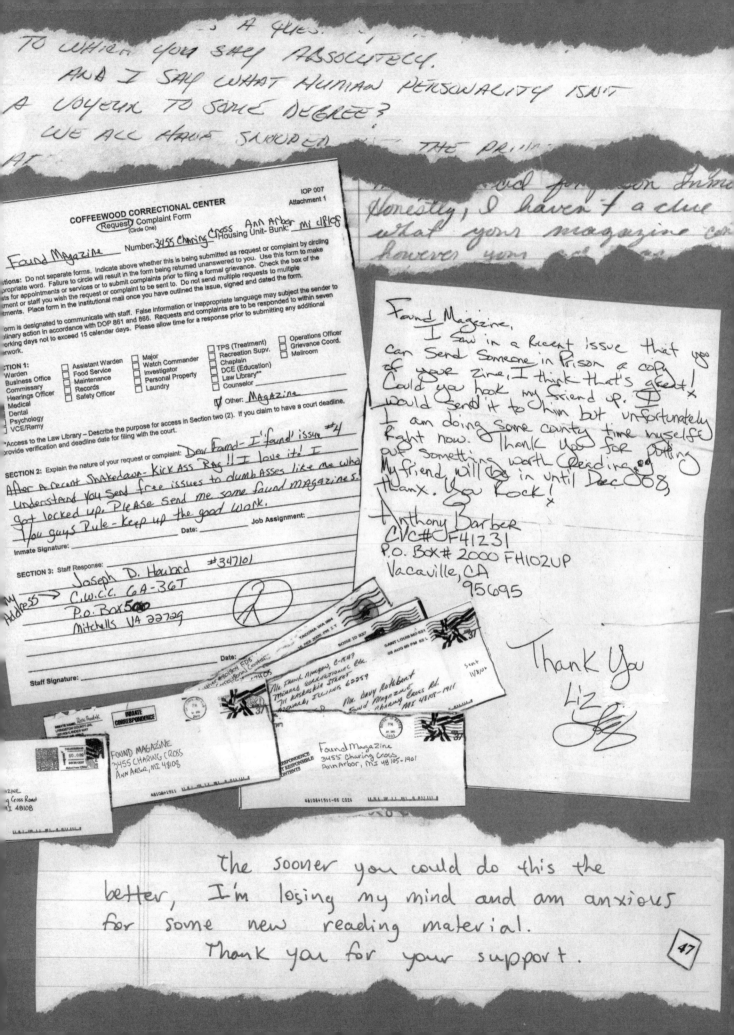

TO WHICH YOU SAY ABSOLUTELY.
AND I SAY WHAT HUMAN PERSONALITY ISN'T
A VOYEUR TO SOME DEGREE?
WE ALL HAVE SHOWED

... A KISS ...

AT ...   THE PRINT ...

... for ... son Inma
Honestly, I haven't a clue
what your magazine con
however you ...

COFFEEWOOD CORRECTIONAL CENTER
(Request) Complaint Form
(Circle One)

IOP 007
Attachment 1

Found Magazine   Number: 3455 Charing Cross Ann Arbor Housing Unit- Bunk: MI 48108

...ctions: Do not separate forms. Indicate above whether this is being submitted as request or complaint by circling ...propriate word. Failure to circle will result in the form being returned unanswered to you. Use this form to make ...sts for appointments or services or to submit complaints prior to filing a formal grievance. Check the box of the ...rtment or staff you wish the request or complaint to be sent to. Do not send multiple requests to multiple ...rtments. Place form in the institutional mail once you have outlined the issue, signed and dated the form.

...form is designated to communicate with staff. False information or inappropriate language may subject the sender to ...plinary action in accordance with DOP 861 and 866. Requests and complaints are to be responded to within seven ...working days not to exceed 15 calendar days. Please allow time for a response prior to submitting any additional ...erwork.

SECTION 1:

☐ Warden
☐ Business Office
☐ Commissary
☐ Hearings Officer
☐ Medical
☐ Dental
☐ Psychology
☐ VCE/Ramy

☐ Assistant Warden
☐ Food Service
☐ Maintenance
☐ Records
☐ Safety Officer

☐ Major
☐ Watch Commander
☐ Investigator
☐ Personal Property
☐ Laundry

☐ TPS (Treatment)
☐ Recreation Supv.
☐ Chaplain
☐ DCE (Education)
☐ Law Library**
☐ Counselor

☐ Operations Officer
☐ Grievance Coord.
☐ Mailroom

☑ Other: Magazine

**Access to the Law Library – Describe the purpose for access in Section two (2). If you claim to have a court deadline, provide verification and deadline date for filing with the court.

SECTION 2: Explain the nature of your request or complaint: Dear Found- I 'found' issue #4 After a recent Shakedown- Kick Ass Rag!! I love it! I understand you send free issues to dumb Asses like me who got locked up. Please send me some found magazines! You guys Rule - keep up the good work.

Date: _____   Job Assignment: _____
Inmate Signature: _____

SECTION 3: Staff Response:
Joseph D. Howard   #347101
C.W.C.C. 6A-36T
P.O. Box 500
Mitchells VA 22729

Date: _____
Staff Signature: _____

INMATE CORRESPONDENCE

FOUND MAGAZINE
3455 CHARING CROSS
Ann Arbor, MI 48108

Mr. Frank Amigon C-1549
Menard Correctional Ctr.
711 Kaskaskia Street
Menard, Illinois 62259

Mr. Davy Rothbart
Found Magazine
Charing Cross Rd.
MI 48108-1911

Found Magazine
3455 Charing Cross
Ann Arbor, MI 48105-1901

Found Magazine,
I saw in a Recent issue that you
can send someone in Prison a copy
of your zine, I think that's great!
Could you hook my friend up. I
would send it to him but unfortunately
I am doing some county time myself
right now. Thank you for putting
out something worth reading.
My friend, will be in until Dec. 2008,
Thanx. You Rock!
Anthony Barber
CVC# F41231
P.O. Box# 2000 FH102UP
Vacaville, CA
95695

Thank You
Liz

---

the sooner you could do this the
better, I'm losing my mind and am anxious
for some new reading material.
Thank you for your support.

er 11, 2007—**Buffalo, NY** » Medaille College, 8 pm, Main Bldg., 716-884-3281 x.174
er 12, 2007—**Toronto, ON** » Dakota Tavern, 7 pm, 249 Ossington Ave., 416-850-4579
er 13, 2007—**Ottawa, ON** » Avant-Garde Bar, 8 pm, 135 Besserer Street, 613-321-8908
er 14, 2007—**Montreal, QC** » details TBA

• September 15, 2007—**Burlington, VT** » The Red Square, 8 pm, 136 Church St., 802-859-8909
• September 16, 2007—**Turners Falls, MA** » The Rendezvous, 2 shows! 8 pm & 10 pm, 78 3rd St., 413-326-1676
• September 17, 2007—**Camden, ME** » details TBA
• September 18, 2007—**City TBA** » details TBA
• September 19, 2007—**Boston, MA (Somerville)** » The Burren, 8 pm, 247 Elm St., Davis Sq., 617-776-6896

• September 20, 2007—**Brooklyn, NY** » Union Hall, 7:30 pm sharp!, 702 Union St. @ 5th Ave., 718-638-4400
• September 21, 2007—**New York, NY** » Upright Citizens Brigade Theater, 8 pm sharp!, 307 W. 26th St., 212-366-9176
• September 22, 2007—**New Haven, CT** » details TBA
• September 23, 2007—**Philadelphia, PA** » details TBA

• September 24, 2007—**Washington, D.C.** » details TBA
• September 24, 2007—**Baltimore, MD** » details TBA
• September 26, 2007—**Boston, MA** » Berklee Performance Center w/ Sarah Vowell, Dave Eggers, details TBA
• September 27, 2007—**Fairfax, VA** » George Mason U., 6 pm, details TBA

• October 9, 2007—**Chicago, IL** » details TBA
• October 11, 2007—**Milwaukee, WI** » Hotcakes Gallery, 8 pm, 3379 N. Pierce St., 414-961-7714
• October 12, 2007—**Madison, WI** » Orpheum Theater, 9 pm, 216 State Street, 608-255-8755
• October 13, 2007—**Omaha, NE** » Bemis Center, 8 pm, 724 S. 12th St., 402-341-7130

• October 14, 2007—**Sioux Falls, SD** » details TBA
• October 15, 2007—**Denver, CO** » details TBA
• October 16, 2007—**Salt Lake City, UT** » SLC Public Library, 7 pm, 210 E. 400 S., 801-322-8133
• October 17, 2007—**Boise, ID** » Visual Arts Collective, 8 pm, address and phone # TBA

• October 19, 2007—**Port Angeles, WA** » details TBA (A.M. event)
• October 23, 2007—**Bothell, WA** » details TBA (at C.C.C.)
• October 24, 2007—**Olympia, WA** » Capitol Theater, time TBA, 206 E. 5th Ave., 36-754-3635
• October 25, 2007—**Seattle, WA** » details TBA
• October 26, 2007—**Portland, OR** » Holocene, 8 pm, 1001 SE Morrison, 503-239-7639

FOUND magazine's THERE GOES THE NEIGHBORHOOD TOUR "2007!"

with **Davy Rothbart** & **Peter Rothbart**

Dang—you *knew* it wasn't safe. And you were right. FOUND Magazine's Davy & Peter Rothbart are back on the road this fall on a 65-city rampage! Davy will drink till his eyes shine with fire and share a trunk-load of sparkling brand-new finds; Peter will play chess in the corner, make the ladies swoon, and blast you with his brand-new jams based on notes in FOUND #5. (From November 12th to December 5th we'll be joined by our partner-in-crime, PostSecret's Frank Warren, who will share his own secrets and armwrestle your mayor. For real.) Can you kick it with us? Yes you can! Come on out and join us for these parties!! Please bring your finds to share, and let your friends in other cities know we're headed their way!!

• October 27, 2007—**Arcata, CA** » details TBA
• October 29, 2007—**Sacramento, CA** » Bodytribe Fitness, 8 pm, 920 21st Street, 916-444-2384
• October 30, 2007—**San Francisco, CA** » details TBA
• November 1, 2007—**Berkeley, CA** » details TBA

• November 2, 2007—**Los Angeles, CA** » details TBA
• November 3, 2007—**San Diego, CA** » details TBA
• November 4, 2007—**Long Beach, CA** » details TBA
• November 6, 2007—**Los Angeles, CA (Hollywood)** » details TBA
• November 7, 2007—**Los Angeles, CA (Westwood)** » details TBA

17149

48

Davy Rothbart

these two photos FOUND by Eric Michael Morris, Hammond, IN

- November 8, 2007—**Tucson, AZ** » Main Library, 12 noon, 101 N. Stone Ave., 520-791-4393
- November 8, 2007—**Tucson, AZ** » Club Congress, 7 pm, 311 E. Congress St., 520-622-8848
- November 9, 2007—**Albuquerque, NM** » Guild Cinema, 8 pm, 3405 Central Avenue NE, 505-255-1848
- November 10, 2007—**Tulsa, OK** » Coffee House on Cherry Street, 8 pm, 1502 E. 15th St, 918-779-6137

- November 12, 2007—**Kansas City, MO** » details TBA
- November 13, 2007—**St. Louis, MO** » Mad Art Gallery, 8 pm, 2727 S. 12th St. (Soulard), 314-771-8230
- November 14, 2007—**Lexington, KY** » details TBA
- November 15, 2007—**Indianapolis, IN** » Big Car Gallery, (2 shows!) 7 pm & 9 pm, 1043 Virginia Ave, 317-408-1366

- November 16, 2007—**Ann Arbor, MI** » Michigan Theater, time TBA, 603 E Liberty Street, 734-668-8463
- November 17, 2007—**Pittsburgh, PA** » Future Tenant, (2 shows!) 7 pm & 9 pm, 821 Penn Ave., 412-325-7037
- November 18, 2007—**Columbus, OH** » Chop Chop Gallery, (2 shows!) 6 pm & 8 pm, 78 Parsons Ave, 614-222-2467

- November 30, 2007—**Asheville, NC** » The Grey Eagle, 8 pm, 185 Clingman Ave., 828-232-5800
- December 1, 2007—**Durham, NC** » Man Bites Dog Theater, (2 shows!) 7 pm & 9:30 pm, 703 Foster St, 919-682-3343
- December 2, 2007—**Richmond, VA** » Firehouse Theater, (2 shows!) 7 pm & 9 pm, 1609 W. Broad St., 804-355-2001

- November 27, 2007—**Pontiac, MI** » details TBA
- November 28, 2007—**Grand Rapids, MI** » details T
- November 29, 2007—**Charleston, WV** » details TBA

- December 3, 2007—**Atlanta, GA** » Push Push Theater, (2 shows!) 7 pm & 9 pm, 121 New St., 404-377-6332
- December 4, 2007—**Birmingham, AL** » Workplay, 8 pm, 500 23rd Street South, 205-879-4773
- December 5, 2007—**New Orleans, LA** » details TBA

- December 7, 2007—**Houston, TX** » Aurora Picture Show, 8 pm, 800 Aurora St., 713-868-2101
- December 8, 2007—**Nacogdoches, TX** » Millard's Crossing, 7 pm, 6020 North, 936-564-6631
- December 9, 2007—**Austin, TX** » Alamo Drafthouse, time TBA, 320 E. 6th St., phone # TBA
- December 10, 2007—**Dallas, TX** » The Public Trust, 8 pm, 2919-C Commerce St., 214-760-7170

- December 11, 2007—**Oklahoma City, OK** » details TBA
- December 12, 2007—**Lawrence, KS** » details TBA

Dates may shift—please stay tuned
to the website for up-to-the-second info!

foundmagazine.com

DUMB DAVY

FOUND by Meg Hopeman

Minneapolis, MN

EVALUATION

Sunday Edition: Davy Rothbart Discusses 'Found'
Downtown-MPR – Sunday, May 8, 2005

1. Overall, how would you rate this program?

(1) 2   3   4   5
Inadequate   Very successful

Comments: *Why do you sware in public so much? It's disrespectful*

2. Where did you hear about this program?

a. Library website _____
b. Posters, bookmarks & flyers in the Library _____
c. Posters outside the Library _____
d. Ann Arbor News Community Events columns _____
e. Axis Teen Newsletter _____
f. Library email notification _____
g. Ann Arbor Observer Events Listings _____
h. Ann Arbor Observer Library Ad _____
i. Current Magazine _____
j. Other newspaper (name) _____
k. Radio ____ m. Cable television _____
l. Other (please explain)
My parents made me

3. How many times have you used the Library system in the last year?
Never ____ Seldom ____ Occasionally ✓ Often ____

4. Was this day/time convenient for you? Yes ✓ No ____
If not, when do you suggest?

5. Do you have any suggestions for future programs?
Don't sware so much you look dumb.

Peter Rothbart

49

*F*inally, Elmer's years of hopeless bungling catch up with him.
J. Edgar Hoover drops the guillotine.

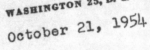

UNITED STATES DEPARTMENT OF JUSTICE
FEDERAL BUREAU OF INVESTIGATION

WASHINGTON 25, D. C.

October 21, 1954

In Reply, Please Refer to
File No.

Mr. Elmer L. Jacobsen
Federal Bureau of Investigation
Kansas City, Missouri

<u>PERSONAL AND CONFIDENTIAL</u>

Dear Mr. Jacobsen:

You are hereby requested to submit your resignation as a Special Agent in the Federal Bureau of Investigation effective at 12:00 noon on October 25, 1954, when your current accrued annual leave expires, active duty having ceased at 3:00 P. M. on October 12, 1954.

This action is being taken in view of a number of serious delinquencies in your performance as disclosed during a recent inquiry into allegations made against you. Specifically, this inquiry disclosed improper handling on your part of an investigative matter, including failure to analyze your objective and channel your efforts accordingly; improper reporting; failure to provide complete details concerning an interview conducted and failure to close the case in question when investigation warranted no further attention. In addition, you were extremely careless in proceeding unarmed on a criminal-type investigation under the circumstances existing. You exercised poor judgment in telephonically obtaining the arrest record of a person interviewed and in discussing this record in the presence of this person and another individual, neither of whom were subjects of the investigation being conducted. You should have been more circumspect in your remarks before these individuals. You also exercised poor judgment in attempting to develop another individual as an informant and in exchanging information with this individual concerning the subject of your investigation. Moreover, your actions in parking in a prohibited area, tying up an office telephone and organizing your investigative notes in this office were most indiscreet.

Furthermore, you erroneously accused an official superior of personal animosity in conducting personnel inquiries and you were presumptuous and disrespectful of the authority of this official superior by demanding to know details of a personnel investigation conducted. It was determined that on one occasion you were inattentive and discourteous at an agent's conference and that on another occasion you either misunderstood or

50

Mr. Elmer L. Jacobsen
Kansas City, Missouri

-2-

deliberately misrepresented an admonition given you by your official superior to insure you were not investigating cases which were not within the investigative jurisdiction of this Bureau. Finally, it was disclosed that since you have been assigned to the Kansas City Office you have been involved in an excessive number of delinquencies including low production, excessive time spent in the office, improper reporting, insufficient attention to an important phase of the Bureau's activities and failure to follow specific Bureau instructions concerning this phase of the Bureau's activities.

Very truly yours,

John Edgar Hoover
Director

3233 Karnes Blvd.
Kansas City, Missouri
October 25, 1954

J. Edgar Hoover, Director
Federal Bureau of Investigation
U. S. Department of Justice
Washington, D.C.

Dear Mr. Hoover:

After considerable thought with regard to the welfare and needs of my family, I very much regret that it is necessary to submit my resignation from the Federal Bureau of Investigation. It will be deeply appreciated if this resignation can be considered effective as of noon, Monday, October 25, 1954.

I do want you to know I have enjoyed the opportunity of working in the Bureau, and feel I have benefited immeasurably from the experience and wide associations it has made possible.

Should the opportunity ever present itself, you are assured that I will gladly render any assistance possible to the Bureau.

Very truly yours,

Elmer L. Jacobsen

Is this the end for our intrepid G-man??

MY LIFE AS A G MAN **CONTINUES**

*E*lmer's crime-fighting days may be numbered, but he ain't
going down without a fight. This heartfelt plea for mercy is,
to me, the centerpiece of the Elmer Jacobsen files.

3233 Karnes Blvd.
Kansas City, Missouri
October 24, 1954

J. Edgar Hoover, Director
Federal Bureau of Investigation
U. S. Department of Justice
Washington, D. C.

Dear Mr. Hoover:

Yesterday evening I did the most difficult
thing I have ever been called upon to do - submit my
resignation from the Federal Bureau of Investigation.

All day today I have been reminding myself
of what I am losing. Therefore, I am directing this
letter to you in a last effort to avoid this catastrophe.

If, during the time I have been under suspension,
October 12 to 22, 1954, I had known that my resignation
was to be requested, the suspension would have been much
more difficult to endure. On November 6, 1954 I was to
celebrate my 15th anniversary in the Bureau. But the
Bureau has been my life longer than that - in fact since
1934 when upon graduation from high school in Minneapolis
I began preparing myself for a career in your service.
During the past fifteen years all I have done, officially
or privately, has been with the welfare of the Bureau
uppermost in my mind. I have always sought your approbation,
and apparently was too zealous in my efforts in this direction during the recent past here at Kansas City.

I realize that I was wrong in accusing an official
superior of being motivated by personal animosity in connection with an investigation of allegations of personal
misconduct on my part.

I also realize now that I apparently placed too
much emphasis on development of informants as compared to
other matters which were also assigned to me.

All my plans and dreams of the past twenty years
have hinged on the Bureau. To have the Bureau taken away

J. Edgar Hoover, Director

10-24-54

from me is no less a blow than to lose a loved one. It is part of my family and part of me. To lose it due to action on my part which appeared to be disrespectful or disloyal is doubly agonizing. I have always had the utmost respect for you and your choice of assistants, and I wish to offer my most sincere apology if my actions of the recent past have left a different impression.

Needless to say I was extremely disappointed in the efficiency report of October 23, 1954 with regard to my work of the past six and one half months. I am positive that I can do satisfactory work for the Bureau, and it is noted that this is the only occasion in nearly fifteen years of service that I have been described as an unsatisfactory employee. I am sure that in a probationary period in your employ I would prove that I am capable and worthy of continued employment by the Federal Bureau of Investigation.

My sorrow at this turn of events is matched only by my determination again to do work that meets with your approval wherever you decide I should be assigned and at whatever salary you believe to be commensurate with my capabilities.

Therefore, in all humility I implore that further consideration be given to retaining me as an employee of the Federal Bureau of Investigation. I realize that in making this request I am in no way changing the recent reports you have received concerning me. However, if it now appears that I may still have a value to the Bureau, and you desire to have this matter further discussed with me, I would gladly appear at Bureau Headquarters, Washington D. C. at my own expense any time I am so directed.

In conclusion, Mr. Hoover, I plead for your forgiveness and for an act of mercy from you. Without it, to be excluded from the Bureau is not only a tremendous blow to me personally but I feel it will have a profound adverse effect on my children, four of whom are of school age and have been extremely proud of the fact that their father is an FBI Agent.

Therefore, I appeal to you personally requesting that my resignation under date of October 23, 1954 not be accepted and that I be restored to duty wherever you may choose as you see fit.

If you can accede to this request, you will forever have the undying gratitude of my wife and me.

Very truly yours,

Elmer L. Jacobsen

A beautiful letter, no doubt. But is it too late for Elmer to save his job?

United States Department of Justice
Federal Bureau of Investigation
Washington 25, D. C.

IN REPLY, PLEASE REFER TO

FILE NO. _____

October 28, 1954

<u>PERSONAL AND CONFIDENTIAL</u>

Mr. Elmer L. Jacobsen
3233 Karnes Boulevard
Kansas City, Missouri

Dear Mr. Jacobsen:

This letter acknowledges receipt of your communication dated October 23, 1954, submitting your resignation as a Special Agent of this Bureau, and your subsequent letter of October 24, 1954, wherein you requested that your resignation as previously submitted not be accepted.

In accordance with your request your resignation is not being accepted; however, in view of the serious derelictions on your part which were pointed out to you in my letter of October 21, 1954, you are being suspended without pay from 3:00 P.M. on October 12, 1954, through November 11, 1954, and placed on probation. In the future you will be expected to show by your attitude and the proper performance of your duties that you are qualified and disposed to remain a Special Agent of this Bureau.

Very truly yours,

John Edgar Hoover
Director

AUG · 55

54

United States Department of Justice
Federal Bureau of Investigation
Washington 25, D. C.

October 28, 1954

IN REPLY, PLEASE REFER TO

FILE NO.

Mr. Elmer L. Jacobsen
Federal Bureau of Investigation
Kansas City, Missouri

Dear Mr. Jacobsen:

Your headquarters are being changed, public business permitting, from Kansas City, Missouri, to Savannah, Georgia, effective upon your arrival there on or after this date.

This change is made for official reasons and not primarily for your convenience or benefit, or at your request. You will be allowed your necessary expenses of transportation and a per diem in lieu of subsistence of $9.00 in connection therewith, such expenses to include the transportation of your immediate family as provided for in Public Law 600 of August 2, 1946, and Executive Order 9805, approved November 25, 1946, as amended.

You are authorized to use a privately owned automobile in connection with your transfer and you will be reimbursed at the rate of seven cents per mile not to exceed the cost of common carrier by the most direct route, plus incidental expenses in connection therewith, of all persons officially traveling in that vehicle. Should your dependents travel by privately owned automobile separate and apart from you, mileage at seven cents per mile is authorized under the same conditions as above.

The transportation of your household goods and personal effects will be paid in accordance with regulations contained in Public Law 600 of August 2, 1946, and Executive Order 9805, approved November 25, 1946, as amended.

Enclosure

Very truly yours,

J. Ea. Hoover
John Edgar Hoover
Director

Apparently not! J. Edgar Hoover shows his soft side, and lets Elmer off the hook with just a month's suspension and reassignment to Savannah, Georgia.

3233 Karnes
Kansas City 11, Missouri
November 4, 1954

Mr. J. Edgar Hoover
Director
Federal Bureau of Investigation
U. S. Department of Justice
Washington, D. C.

Dear Mr. Hoover:

Mere words cannot fully express my appreciation for your kindness in restoring me to duty as of November 12, 1954. Please be assured that I will be returning to work firmly resolved to prove to you that I am a fully qualified special agent and that I am disposed to remain in this category.

Should my future services to this Bureau be of such character that it becomes desirable to have me advance in the service, the Bureau will find me completely willing to accept any additional responsibilities.

Very truly yours,

Elmer L. Jacobsen
Special Agent

· AUG · 55

Elmer's dodged a cannonball and is back in the Bureau's good graces. But how much longer will he last?

MY LIFE AS A G MAN **CONTINUES ON PAGE** 76

BLUE LINE PERIOD

FOUND by Tim Haldeman

Chicago, IL

A bum sleeping on the Blue Line El train was arrested by the police for sleeping. As the two policemen began to remove him, the bum said, "May I please take my artwork?" The police simply laughed at the old, dirty bum, and dragged him from the train. These drawings were left behind.
—T.H.

57

FINDER SPOTLIGHT
Kimya Dawson

DAVY EXPLAINS!

The music of Kimya Dawson is a huge favorite here at FOUND Magazine HQ. Her songs are both sweet and sad, kind of like a lot of the FOUND notes we receive. So I was thrilled—though not all that surprised—to discover that Kimya is a passionate finder herself. I talked to Kimya in her new hometown of Olympia, Washington, while she played with her baby daughter, Panda.

Davy: Hiya Kimya. So, what've you found for me lately?

Kimya: I just found a piece of paper with only two words on it. First it said "Dere"—but that was crossed out. And below that, it said "Deer"—but that was crossed out, too. And that was it. The paper was just crumpled up on the ground. The poor soul couldn't spell "Dear"—they gave up. That made me so sad. Someone had something really nice to say to somebody and they couldn't even start.

Davy: Do you remember the first thing you ever found?

Kimya: One of my first finds—I was, like, five years old—and I found my neighbor's glass eye. That was pretty scary. There was this older kid up the street—Jimmy McKinstry—he was kind of Dungeon Master-y; he was like a pre-Trenchcoat-Mafia Trenchcoat Mafia type of kid. Always wore a black trenchcoat, had kinda long hair. Him and another kid in the neighborhood had been playing up the street—with BB guns, of course—and he got shot in the eye and lost his eye.

Well, growing up, my brother and I used to do these carnival things in the backyard all the time. We'd charge kids a penny to throw a rock through a tire to win a prize, and if they won we'd give out pinecones or popcorn or paper airplanes. Jimmy McKinstry must've been looking in our money can, and I guess his eye fell out, but he didn't see where it went. Later, I was counting money and I found his eye. I just remember shouting, *"There's an eyeball in the pennies!!"* And Jimmy came rushing over, like, "Damn, there it is!" and stared at me all accusingly with his gaping socket.

Davy: Dang, haha, I'm glad he was reunited with his eye. Do you remember other early finds of yours?

Kimya: Well, I've always been kind of obsessed with pictures of people I don't know. Families. Kids. Old men. I used to work in the library in my town. Part of my reason for wanting to work there was all the years and years of archived yearbooks. I would just be like, "Yeah, I'm gonna go organize this back room, guys, gotta shelve some books," and then I'd sit and look through old yearbooks for hours, year by year, seeing how people had aged over the years. I've always had this obsession with getting glimpses of people I don't know and trying to imagine their story. That's why I love finding pictures. I love just absorbing the expressions on people's faces—they're totally caught in that moment. I found a Polaroid once of a fat kid in a tight T-shirt flexing his muscles, and that was one of my favorite pictures I ever found. He was just so *happy*; he was like, "Whoa-*ohhhh*—look at my biceps!"

Davy: I feel like in found photos, someone's expression can reveal so much—you don't know the details of what's happening in that moment, but their face, their *eyes*, say everything. Like maybe everyone's happy in a picture, but one person has this kind of sad and lost look.

Kimya: Yeah, especially in candid pictures of people, something poignant so often gets captured. They were just thinking about something, and someone caught 'em. It's sort of the same as peeking in someone's window—we all do that, too... right?

Davy: I've never passed a lit-up window and not looked in.

illustration by Brendt Rioux

Kimya: We don't necessarily stop and stare, but I'll always glance inside... I'm like, "Hey, what's going on in *there*?" Yeah, finding pictures is cool, but I think I kind of prefer finding notes. I always want to find a full-on *letter*. Once I found a letter that some teenage girl was writing, a breakup letter. But I imagine it was the rough draft. It was really, really abrasive. And sad. It was written in blue colored-pencil, everything was misspelled, and it was very emotional.

Davy: Around here, we see all kinds of breakup letters people have found and sent in. Some are emotional off the bat. Then some, they're small-talking the first page and a half or so, and then they drop the bomb. More often, we see the kinds of letters where people are nervous about their relationship, asking why someone's been distant. They always beat around, and then...

www.foundmagazine.com

Millions of finds!

(Okay, not millions. But a lot. Like several thousand.)

Kimya: I know, I know! They're nervous, so they try to sneak it in there: "Why didn't you call me on Saturday? Is something wrong? Did I do something wrong? Do you still love me?"

CONTINUED ON NEXT PAGE!

Davy: Exactly. Hey, do you have an all-time favorite find?

Kimya: I think the centerpiece of my collection is a really great find that was gifted to me. A friend of mine found a big manila envelope full of photocopied letters that 4th- and 5th-graders had written to The Rock. The wrestler. It was amazing, these city kids pouring their hearts out to him about why he's their hero. "Dear The Rock, you inspire me…" I'm always wondering: did The Rock write back?

Davy: Years ago, kids wrote to Santa Claus, and opened up their stories to him, but now it's The Rock.

Kimya: Yeah, it was like a class project—the whole class wrote letters to The Rock. Some of them were just like, "Hey The Rock, you're so strong! I think it's really cool that you kick butt." And some of them were like, "I don't have a dad. I wish you were my dad. You seem really nice. And I want someone like you to take care of me." Really anguished ones and then ones like, "Oh, that match you had against Stone Cold Steve Austin was so cool." Sometimes both hues in the same letter. "I want you to be my dad because you kick ass, and I don't have a dad."

Davy: What kinds of emotions do you go through when reading letters like that

Kimya: I just feel like I won a prize. Heh heh. It really is like finding treasure. A special kind of treasure. The notes can make you sad, but they're also really exciting.

Davy: It's like the closest you can be to a stranger you'll never meet. You can imagine them hovering over this letter, pressing down with their pen… they become so alive.

illustration by Brendt Rioux

Kimya: It's almost like you're *inside* them. Seeing through their eyes for a minute. It's one of the most exciting feelings in life. I guess some people think it's too voyeuristic to read other people's letters—that it's just plain wrong—but I don't think it is. It would be wrong if there was an address and phone number, and I called the person and was like, "Ooooh, I can't believe you said this." If I tried to get involved. But I think just reading something a stranger wrote and dropped is okay. It's tough, though, 'cause I've written really awkward diaries myself. Now I journal everything online and I have no shame, but there's journals from when I was 16 that I wouldn't want anyone to see. I used to write letters to Sting. I filled entire journals with letters to Sting.

Davy: So Sting was your The Rock?

Kimya: Yeah, hahaha. Sting was my The Rock. I think this one letter, it's the only thing I have in my life I'm not comfortable sharing with the world. Maybe someday. But whenever I think of this one particular letter and poem I wrote to Sting, I feel really, really uncomfortable. If someone found that, I might die. It's a good reminder to me to be sensitive when I'm reading other people's stuff, to be sure I'm laughing along with them, and not laughing *at* them.

Davy: I shouldn't ask, but, I mean… why was this one letter so…?

Kimya: It wasn't a sexy letter or anything. I was pretty young and he was really old. I think I just got way too heavy. Talking about the way his saxophone player had inspired me. *Really* awkward.

Davy: Do you know where that letter is now? Or is it floating around somewhere it could be found?

Kimya: No, I know exactly where that letter is. It's accompanied by a lot of pencil sketches of him. Sting, that is. Okay, and the saxophonist, too. Really, though, when I think about it, I lose more stuff than I find. I lose *everything*—wallets, keys, backpacks—everything!

Davy: Haha, yeah, I'm the same way. Anything you lost that hurt particularly?

Kimya: I had a Curious George I lost when I was little and that was really, really sad. Then once I left my Paddington Bear on the bus, and me and my mom had to find the main bus depot and track him down. It's funny, because Paddington Bear, he was an orphan, you know; in the original story, he was found at Paddington station. Well, when we got to the bus station, the folks there had set him up like he was typing at a typewriter. I was so happy to see him!

And then years later I had this weird experience of losing stuff—I had a bunch of stuff in storage in this one town, and then I moved, but still intended on going back for it, and then a friend of mine found all my stuff from the storage locker at the free store in that town. They saw a New Kids on the Block lunchbox with my name on it, and called me, like, "Um…yo… I found all of your possessions."

Davy: Did you race down and try to get your stuff back?

KIMYA DAWSON

REMEMBER THAT I ♥ YOU

Kimya: No, I'm kind of a pack rat, so when I lose stuff, if it's not my passport, I just kinda let it go. I can always find new stuff to replace what I've lost. The world is full of giant clocks and strange letters and pink spoons and beautiful Polaroids waiting to be discovered. I've got boxes and boxes of crap. Every time I find something, I'm like, "Oh! I need this forever!"

Kimya Dawson's albums include *My Cute Fiend Sweet Princess, Hidden Vagenda,* and *Remember That I Love You.* Check out her music, tour info, (non-Sting-related) journals, and lots more neat stuff at **www.kimyadawson.com**.

[special thanks to Amber Bua at K Records]

DAVY ROTHBART
&
FRANK WARREN
PRESENT:
FOUND VS. POSTSECRET
LIVE "2007!" TOUR
november 12 – kansas city, MO
november 13 – st. louis, MO
november 14 – lexington, KY
november 15 – indianapolis, IN
november 16 – ann arbor, MI
november 17 – pittsburgh, PA
november 18 – columbus, OH
november 30 – asheville, NC
december 1 – durham, NC
december 2 – richmond, VA
december 3 – atlanta, GA
december 4 – birmingham, A
december 5 – new orleans, LA
dates may shift.
check online!
SHOP 24 HOURS A DAY!
THANK YOU FOR SHOPPI
finds!
secrets!
arm-wrestling!
music, magic & mayhem!
much more info at:
www.foundvspostsecret.com
www.postsecret.com
www.poemadept.com
www.foundmagazine.com
events will benefit local charities in each city.
found & postsecret will make separate visits to dozens of other cities in the fall of 2007 – check online for details!

6-17-08 ①

I hope this letter Reaches you in the best of Health and spirit's.

Hey baby I won't ask how you are doing because that would be ~~stupid~~ - I'm sitting here with you all on my mind - I called your mom and spoke with her about 4 times and explain your situation to her - I don't know if she's gonna bond you out or not - But I hope she does - she's checking some stuff out so whenever she takes care of her bussiness - then she probly will make some arrangments to get you out - I love you Cheesa Crisp and miss you so much on the Real girl - My mom says that she loves you and miss you not - I called the phone company and got the block tooken off O.K. - Here is a picture to help you get through these fuck up days - always Remember that I'm on your side O.K. - when you start to feel lonely or sad - Just be strong and hold your Head up and look at the picture of me and hope it will bring a smile apon your face -

②

And always know one thing Cheesa - the dude that's the tallest in the picture is your dude baby always - you don't have to worry - you know that you got this big dick on lock down - don't you know that I aint nobody can put it down on me the way you do baby - My eyes all watery and shit - I need my baby here with me -

Well my finest - I'm gonna try to get some sleep - which is so hard to do without you beside me.

"Call me"
think of me always.
Probent

smell your dude

this photo FOUND by Capella Mearer, Cockeysville, MD

006

63

A Write in Candidate For Sheriff Democrat

VOTE LeRoy Lieurance as your next Sheriff

Born and Raised in Torrington Wyo.
Enployed by Holly Sugar since 1981
A member of The First Free will Baptists Church
A Family man that's conserned about the way

This county has been ran, Thats why its Time For

a new change in office

He desided at a early age to Follow in his heros
Foot Steps, Herald Dewitt, Matt Dillin, J.F. Kennady,
all great men, that earn the Respect of the peaple, and
Thats the way LeRoy Lieurance wants to run the

Sheriff's Department,
For The peaple, to serve and protect the peaple.
Give LeRoy Lieurance A chance to prove himself.
Sinserly
Mrs. Lieurance

WRITE-IN

FOUND by Mike Richman & Monte Pickett

Cheyenne, WY

We learned from friends who live near Torrington, Wyoming tha
LeRoy Lieurance runs for Sheriff every election cycle. We've
always wondered: Is Mrs. Lieurance his wife or his mother?

—M.R. & M.P.

"Recalls Fitzgerald and Kerouac... Rothbart's characters dare to seek adventure."
—Justin Clark, *L.A. Weekly*

"Beautiful... Rothbart finds poetry, dignity and oddity in the mundane and fleeting moments of everyday life."
—**Philadelphia City-Paper**

"Davy writes with his whole heart. These stories are crushing."
—ARTHUR MILLER

THE LONE SURFER OF MONTANA, KANSAS

STORIES

DAVY ROTHBART
AUTHOR OF THE NATIONAL BESTSELLER *FOUND*

PRAISE FOR THE LONE SURFER OF MONTANA, KANSAS

"Funny, flashy... a great whirlwind."
—*The Los Angeles Times*

"It is storytelling at its simplest and at its finest... a blend of melancholy and bravado. It's the pleasure of Rothbart's writing that each yarn begins with a moment that feels so real and yet so out of the ordinary that you're hooked from the opening scene."
—Alex Kotlowitz, *Chicago Tribune*

"Like Kerouac's best novels, these stories are breezy and energetic dispatches from obscure corners of the country.... Rothbart mines his material to heartbreaking effect."
—**The Washington Post**

Available wherever books are sold.

"A quirky, perceptive volume..."
—**Entertainment Weekly**

"Witty and heartfelt as well as salty and somber, it's a 162-page romp—eight pieces of short fiction featuring folks who don't always make the best decisions, but somehow, as Bruce Springsteen once put it, come to the end of every hard-earned day with a reason to believe."
—John Mark Eberhart, *Kansas City Star*

"It's always exciting to discover a talented new writer. Davy writes with such energy, wit, and heart."
—**Judy Blume**

FIRESIDE
A Division of Simon & Schuster
A CBS COMPANY

"Stunning and intimate... Rothbart shines a light on America's underbelly."
—The Boston Phoenix

"Provocative, original, and potent—at one moment hilarious, at the next heartbreaking... robust with flavor... we're left yearning for more."
—Elle

"A truly wonderful and daring first collection."
—The Grand Rapids (Mich.) Press

CAREER CRIMINAL

FOUND by Brian Williams

Ann Arbor, MI

This portion of a letter was found in my back yard. I can only imagine what prompted the letter to be written.   —B.W.

Have you ever been to jail, or been arrested? I know you get introuble for your liscence, but I don't think you get arrested. I was arrested the first time. 3-16-1991 for 2 counts of C.C.W. & 1 count Retail Fraud II degree. (C.C.W. stands for carrying a conceald weapon.) let's see 1991, that would make me 14 years old. I remember that day, I got busted stealing a carton of Lucky strikes, I had a 25cal. (wich is a small hand gun) and a switch blade on me. I only know the date 'cause I have a copy of my rap sheet here. Ive been arrested - total of 26 times. I have. 9 felonies & 3 misdemeanors on my Juvinile. & 6 felonies & 6 misdemeanors on my adult record. I also have 3 felonies I had droped, wich they couldn't convict me of due to lack of evidence. All & all it's a pretty extensive criminal record. They lable me as a career criminal. wich is true, I guess. shit I still have that warrent in Ah, so + 1 more misdemeanors to that eventualy. Wow - I'm a fuck up. So here's the list of everyplace Ive lived that I can remember. I was born in Detroit, @ Hutzel Hospital on Woodward in the Cass Corridore. 2 foster homes I can't remember. Then my foster mom & Dad's. We lived on Fernbrook in Troy, & then Moved to Cardinal in Troy. I left @ 12 due to the beating's & emotinal abuse. I was in the Juvinile home @ 14, @ 15 I ran, & lived on the streets again, then w/ this friend & his mom for a bit. I got busted. went back to jeuvnile to a Maximum security level. 1½

Years later I left, then I went to some hikery thig 'n Twinfall Idaho for a month. Then off to St. Lake City Utah for boarding school. I came back when I was 16½ or 17. Kathy got pregnate 'f I lived on her Mom's couch. Some how I ended up in my Mom's basement for a month or so, then I lived in a basement of a friend (more like a brother) 5 houses down the street. a few months later I rented a room, no back up. I stayed on another friend's mom's couch for a month or so, then I rented a room out of the newspaper. I lived w/ 2 guys. Much older & one guys x-wife. then my truck, then that x-wife let me stay @ her new place when she moved out. I fucked that up & my truck died so, I lived on the streets for about 4-5 months, which sucked it was like Jan - April. I used to sleep under cars, park's, abanded build's ect. Then I got another place. Fucked that up. back to a friends couch. Then rehab, the streets, Jail, the streets. Then I lived w/ this lady named Harley. She was some biker. Then w/ this guy shawn & a couple people. Then homeless, & I traveled w/ this girl & saw alot of concerts. We lived in her van. Then back to MI. Homeless, then my boy "E" let me stay. Then me & "E" moved to pontiac from Royal Oak. we had a few places togeather. Then outta a while lot of going in & out of jail while I lived w/ "E". Then I met Liz. We had 2 places in pontiac, then one in berkley, then 1 in ferndale. I also went to jail on & off then. Then. I lived in my truck 'f homeless. Then my aunt Pam let me stay for a min. Then homeless. Then in Yipsi w/ a friend. Then Jail for 13½ months. ¾ house, Then me & Liz got

FOUND Magazine.
I still have that warrant in A2.

67

San Francisco Police Department
NARRATIVE

060729579

On 07/10/06 my partner Off Gibbs #1493 and i were in plain clothes in an unmarked police vehicle. We were conducting surveillance in and around the Mission corridor between 29th Street and Cesar Chavez. Based on our training and experience we know this area to have high rates of narcotics activities at all hours of the day and night. We have made numerous narcotics arrests in and around the area.

At approximately 1330 hours I was in an undisclosed location with a clear and unobstructed view of the 3100 block of Mission Street, when I observed (B) Dean walking S/B on Mission from Cesar Chavez. Dean walked up to a known narcotics dealer and engaged him in brief conversation. The narcotics dealer nervously looked around, then huddled closer to Dean as the two conducted a hand to hand transaction. Dean then started walking N/B along Mission Street, and into a corner store on Mission and 26th Street where Dean was out of my sight for a short period of time.

At 2974 Mission Street I verbally identified myself as a police officer and placed Dean in handcuffs. Dean told me that he was on parole for narcotics possession.

Computer query confirmed that Dean was on Parole and revealed that Dean had an outstanding No Bail P.A.L. warrant for his arrest.

Officer Gibbs and I were unable to find any narcotics on Dean's person.

3H2C transported Dean to Ingleside Station.

Martin #17 of CWB confirmed the warrant.

Dean was subsequently booked at Ingleside Station on the above listed warrant as approved by Sgt. Jean #935.

As Dean's (P1) computer scanner, was too large to be kept with his personal property, I booked it into evidence at Ingleside Station for safekeeping.

FRONT

BACK

DEAN'S LIST
FOUND by Cris Cowan
San Francisco

I found this police report on Mission Street. On the back, Dean (I presume) has scrawled a ton of nearly illegible thoughts, starting out like this: "I wanna get back to my innocence—my pristineness." He continues on, raging against consumer culture and warmongering politicians, and praying for spiritual salvation and release from chemical addiction. I wonder: did he ever get his scanner back? —C.C.

BOLT ACTION
FOUND by Kristin Riggs
Sacramento, CA

Is it possible to get me, out of here while I fi this case? Preferably now. What about 100,000 Bail reduction If I agree to do 5yrs verificat Longlonico or my uncle?

What can I do about my wife abusing the resta order? She has a history of abusing protective orders.

What can I do about all of the things that the sheriff's dept stole from me, bolt action coins

When can I set my stuff back from them? I have receipts for 90.00 of it.

Can I sue the County for all of this? If so will you help me? Your ower loss of everything lonewife

What about my 50 caliber BMG—April 30 registered deadline?

Do you handle any financ stuff? Will you help me

68

From *Wm. Wright* #53625   *Nov. 8, 1952*   INSPECTED
(Date)   4

To *Mr. Jacobson*, F.B.I. Agent, *U.S. Dept. Justice, Fed. Bldg.*
(Name)   (Address)
        Omaha, Neb.

Dear Sir:

    I wrote a letter to the Marshal of Omaha, Neb. about three weeks ago, to give to you concerning the clothes that you pack from the apartment I was living at the time I was arrested by you and also the clothes and tools that was in the trunk of the car.

    While I was in jail in Omaha, you said that my things were ready to ship but you never said when you would have them shipped. My brother has checked with the post office and express office a number of times in Rock Island, Ill.

    If you still have my things there will you please ship them to ~~Mrs~~ Mrs. Lola Worthington, 2931-14th ave., Rock Island, Ill.

           Yours Truly

           Wm. Wright
           Reg. No. 53625

Wm. Wright #53625

MY SHIT BACK
FOUND by Eric Michael Morris
Hammond, IN

POLICE OFFICERS' ASSOCIATION
OF NEBRASKA

This Is To Certify

ELMER L. JACOBSEN

Special Agent, F.B.I.

Is a Member in good standing

Regular Member

JOSEPH T. CARROLL
SECRETARY-TREASURER

69

JOE COOK
PRESIDENT

"Even though I'm in prison, I'm still a normal person!"

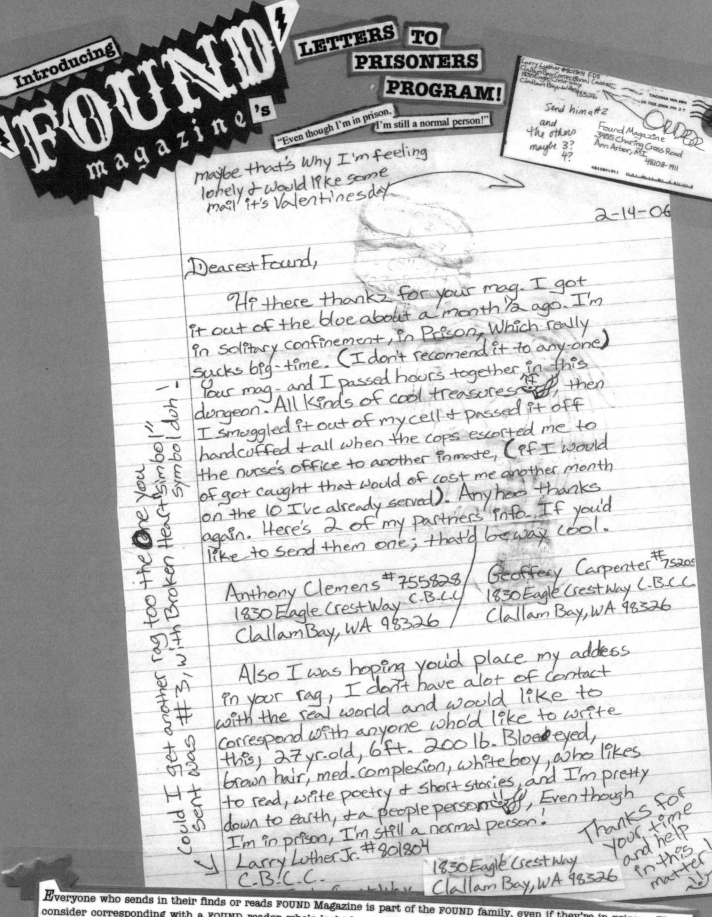

[envelope notes:] Larry Luther #801804 FD8 / Clallam Bay Correctional Center / 1830 Eagle Crest Way / Clallam Bay, WA 98326

Send him #2 and the others maybe 3? 4?

Found Magazine 3455 Charing Cross Road Ann Arbor, MI 48108-1911

ORDER

maybe that's Why I'm feeling lonely & would like some mail it's Valentinesday

2-14-06

Dearest Found,

Hi there thankz for your mag. I got it out of the blue about a month 1/2 ago. I'm in solitary confinement, in Prison, Which really sucks big-time. (I don't recomend it to any-one) Your mag- and I passed hours together in this dungeon. All Kinds of cool treasures 🙂, then I smuggled it out of my cell & passed it off handcuffed & all when the cops escorted me to the nurse's office to another inmate, (if I would of got caught that would of cost me another month on the 10 I've already served). Anyhoo thanks again. Here's 2 of my partners' info. If you'd like to send them one; that'd be way cool.

Anthony Clemens #755828 C-B.C.C. 1830 Eagle Crest Way Clallam Bay, WA 98326

Geoffery Carpenter #75205 1830 Eagle Crest Way C-B-C-C Clallam Bay, WA 98326

Also I was hoping you'd place my address in your rag, I don't have a lot of contact with the real world and would like to correspond with anyone who'd like to write this; 27 yr-old, 6 ft. 200 lb. Blue eyed, brown hair, med. complexion, white boy, who likes to read, write poetry & short stories, and I'm pretty down to earth, & a people person 🙂, Even though I'm in prison, I'm still a normal person!

Larry Luther Jr. #801804 C-B:C-C. 1830 Eagle Crest Way Clallam Bay, WA 98326

Could I get another rag too the one you sent was #3, with Broken Heart symbol "the one you symbol doh -

Thanks for your time and help in this matter!

Everyone who sends in their finds or reads FOUND Magazine is part of the FOUND family, even if they're in prison. Please consider corresponding with a FOUND reader who's locked up! It's really easy—just e-mail us to indicate your interest [info@foundmagazine.com] and we will pass you the name and address of someone in jail who'd be very happy to hear from you. Inmates: interested in trading letters with a FOUND reader on the outside? Just drop us a note and we'll find you a pen pal.

Thanks in advance to everyone who chooses to participate!! —DAVY

Jennifer L ~~~~~~
5285 ~~~~~~ DR. ~~
Cleveland, TN. 37312
Friday, October 28, 2005
Human resource development institution
816 16th street
Washington DC.

Dear Human resource development institution ,

My Husband is now incarcerated at Brushy Mountain Correctional Compound, in Petros TN. With in the last few months the doctor has been keeping an eye on him. His white blood cells have been to high as well as his liver enzymes. They have also done a EKG and found his heart beats to slow. My husband was informed while he was in Taft Youth Development Center, that he needed a new vaive for his heart. I have requested the records from them and I will inform my husband that he needs to release them to me. Last week my husband's heart started to hurt. He broke out in sweats and fell to the floor, before he fell he pushed the call button It took them 20 minutes or so before they came to see what was going on with him. He wrote a grievance and ever since they have been finding crazy ways to get him in trouble. This is the first time in a year that he has been written up, it is not right to be treated that way for seeking help. I realize that it is hard to move people quickly for the fact that the prison system if over crowded. Heart trouble is not some thing that can wait. To most he is a number 343750, but to me he is so much more. I know my husband did wrong, he as well as the others that have done a crime must pay for there actions. But he shouldn't have to pay with his life. Maybe he will make it, maybe he wont. That something to be left in Gods hands. I as his wife made a promise to him to be a voice, were he cant be one. My husband fears that he will die in prison just as his mother did a little over a year ago. September-17-04 Kathy D. Morgan- ~~~~~~ died under the care of the woman's facility in Nashville TN. Her mother tried all she could to help, but never were her pleas answered. The doctor even told us, were ever she was didn't give her proper care. I come to you to day to ask, if there is any way you can help us. I don't expect my husband to be released, but help for what is wrong with him before it is to late. We can't go through B.M.C.C, because of what I informed you already in this letter. I hope to here from y'all soon. Thanks so much for your time!
Sincerely,
Jennifer A~~~~~~
My number is 423-~~~~~~ or 423-~~~~~~ if you have any questions.
My husbands name is Casey Lee A~~~~~~ 343750
Thanks again!!!!

36891
10-13-45
MPLS

71

Dear Kathy,
I did NOT
LEAVE ANYTHING
OUT ON ANYTHING
I CHECKED THE
SEAT BEFORE, getting up
DURING & AFTER.
BESIDES THEY HAD
ALREADY ARRESTED
HIM SO DON'T →

BLAME ME FOR
CHOICES HE Made
HIMSELF. FURTHER-
MORE HE PUT ME,
YOU & NICHOLAS
IN FURTHER DANGER
By telling ME 2 PARK
THERE — WHETHER
HE KNEW IT OR NOT
Thank you for
all your help please don't push me away
as a friend

this photo FOUND by Daniel Costello, Denver, CO

72

9-16-05

To whom This may concern

I'm Just writting to let you know
that claudiette is a very good person
and deserves to be out of Jail

this newspaper clipping
FOUND by Eric Michael Morris, Hammond, IN
(from the files of Elmer Jacobsen)

Cop' Directs Traffic; No Irate Remarks

Grand Island, Mich. (U.P.)—Police caught a snowman directing traffic Wednesday night. Somebody had erected the snowman in the middle of an intersection. It looked so much like a traffic cop that drivers were obeying its arm signal to turn.

precaution... ...zgerald a
said he will file a claim agains...
...he estate.

...Tonigh...

:0.03-D]

...e following act(s) which create an immediate and present
...ore threats or other pattern of conduct which causes you to
...causes or has caused mental distress to you or a family or
...ctions of Respondent for the crime of Menacing by Stalking, if
...:

...e She's gonna kill me
...d with me unaware until
...where I'm at And who I'm with
...s broken out my van windshield
...Publicly Embarasses me threatens
...throws bricks At my van o my ex-wifes van
...t me Sometime or Run me over with
...ed that many times As well.

...r Ohio Revised Code 2903.214 for the safety and protection of the
...amed in this Petition by granting a civil Stalking Protection Order

...titioner and the family of household members named in this
...eatening, molesting, following, stalking, bothering, harassing,
...s upon them.

...ce, school, business, place of employment, or day
...ars named in this Petition, including the

To whom it may Concern, before I proceed any further, I would like to introduce myself as Troy Finona, I'am 25 years old born and raised in the island of Guam and on oahu (HI) where I presently live with my parents.
On the 18th day of march 1998 in the city and County of HI. I was charged for robbery in the 2nd degree, for getting into a fight at a club. He started the trouble to begin with and I just embarressed him in front of his girlfriend and her friends by knocking him out cold fast. Then I found myself being interrogated for hours, and I was intoxicated and also tired. I wanted to go home and sleep but they just kept giving me a hard time, so then I just thought that if I agree with them I'll get out of there faster. That was the worst mistake I have ever made in my life cause now I'm paying for something I agreed to but didn't commit.
As for my driving abstract violations I have only one simple answer its because I was young and careless not knowing

It'll hurt me later in life, but for the mistakes I've made I have learned a valuable lesson from them. But that was then, my life is no longer that way now. If I get the opportunity to Join the army, I would really make a big impact on how much Better my life would be and how much more I can do with my life. and it's been one of my goals since high school that now I can finally complete, and be the best I can possibly be.

73

FOUND INTERVIEW
Mark Bowden

What would you do if you found a million dollars?

On February 26, 1981, a young, unemployed dockworker in Philadelphia named Joey Coyle faced that enormous question. Hanging out with a couple of friends, Joey drove down a little-used alleyway, and found $1.2 million in cash that had fallen out of an armored truck. *Finders Keepers* is author Mark Bowden's riveting account of the weeks that followed. I spoke to him recently about Joey Coyle's wild ride.

Davy: Okay, Mark, back it up for a second. How'd all this cash end up sitting in an alley?

Mark: The armored truck must've hit a pothole, and I guess the back doors weren't securely fastened. Joey drove by a few minutes later and saw a big metal tub in the road and thought it might make a good toolbox. Inside the tub, he found two sacks of money—$800,000 in the first, $400,000 in the second. It was beyond belief. Joey was young, broke, addicted to meth. He spent the next two weeks doing everything *he* thought would enable him to keep the money, when in fact it was everything that ensured he'd be caught.

Davy: So, what would Joey do? What *did* Joey do?

Mark: It's kind of funny in a way. I asked a detective who'd worked on the case: what would be the smart thing to do if you wanted to keep the money? He said, 'Put it in your closet. Don't touch it for a while. And don't tell anyone!' Joey Coyle did the exact opposite. He ran around spending a lot of it; he bragged to everyone he encountered that he was the one who'd found the money, then bribed them not to tell. He thought some of his friends with connections to the Mob could help him launder the money, and passed a huge chunk of it to them, thinking he'd get it back—of course, he never saw another penny of that.

Late one night, drunk, looking for a friend in New Jersey, he stumbled into the wrong house. He talked for a while with the old couple who lived there, promised that he'd help them pay off their mortgage, and left them with a few hundred-dollar bills, asking them to keep things quiet, trying to cover his tracks. Joey was a nut, though in his own way he was lovable. He was a complete fuckup, but he was so inept—so endearingly inept—you just wanted to protect him.

Davy: It kind of makes you wonder what you would do if it was you that found the money. I like to think I could keep it hush-hush enough to get away with it, but who knows? It seems like such a life-changing event. Mark, what do you think *you* would've done?

Mark: I'm the kind of guy, when I find twenty bucks on the street I look around to see who might've dropped it. Joey Coyle was 26- or 27-years-old when he found the money. They were offering a substantial reward—not a million bucks—but a decent amount. I would've given it back and collected the reward. But at that age, I had every expectation that I'd achieve a certain level of success and comfort. A lot of it depends on where you are in life, and if you feel that life has treated you fairly. Joey Coyle believed that life had handed him a raw deal. He had very few prospects; he felt like a total failure. He was addicted to drugs, and wanted things he couldn't have—a job, a girlfriend, a stronger relationship with his family, money. Nothing worked. Here, gloriously, was the answer. Or so he thought.

WORLD BOOK map
Philadelphia Is Located in Southeastern Pennsylvania.

foundmagazine.com

Davy: Yeah, sometimes when you find something amazing, it feels almost cosmic, like the universe has guided it into your hands.

Mark: More specifically, Joey felt like his dead father had given it to him. He thought his relatives in heaven were looking after him. He felt lucky for the first time in his life.

Davy: So what ended up happening?

Mark: After a couple of weeks, the cops finally caught up with him. He was arrested at LaGuardia Airport with $200,000 stuffed in his clothes, trying to fly to Acapulco. He was charged with several crimes. The story of Joey Coyle and the missing million dollars was a *huge* story in Philadelphia. The whole city was caught up in it. An image of him emerged as a lovable folk hero, a Robin Hood type. The truth was a bit darker. He was a meth addict. He spent a week high as a kite, desperately trying to pay everyone off not to turn him in.

Davy: Is there a law about returning FOUND money?

Mark: In Pennsylvania, if you find anything more than $250, you've got to make an effort to return it, or you're subject to criminal prosecution. It's looked at the same as theft. Of course, when Joey's case came to trial, everyone in the city was asking themselves that same question you asked: 'What would *I* do?' It's such an interesting, universal question. And plenty of people thought they'd do the same thing and try to keep the dough. The money came from a casino and was headed to a federal bank. It's not like stealing from someone's grandma. I feel like the situation really challenged folks' moral judgment. There was a lot of sympathy for Joey Coyle. After the jury acquitted him, they shook his hands, hugged and kissed him. "We'd have done the same thing," they told the judge.

Davy: What happened after Joey's trial ended?

Mark: He became a cult celebrity in Philadelphia. But it was extremely hard on him—he was ashamed of himself and the life he was leading; being a celebrity troubled and haunted him. People wanted to make him into this folk hero, but he couldn't play the part, and he knew it. He had more trouble with the law; he was in and out of rehab.

A Hollywood movie was made based on his story, starring John Cusack as Joey, along with James Gandolfini, Benicio Del Toro, Michael Madsen, and Philip Seymour Hoffman. Well, Joey killed himself a couple of weeks before the movie was set to be released. I think the flood of media attention he was about to face when the movie came out truly terrified him.

Davy: Fuck, dude. That's no Hollywood ending.

Mark: I think, ultimately, his story is a story of addiction, the story of someone trying to find a shortcut to happiness. It's one of the classic dreams we all have—to find the pot of the gold at the end of the rainbow. It's a seductive idea that we'll be able to stumble upon one thing in our life—money, or maybe love—and suddenly find happiness. That's what drugs are all about, providing that shortcut to bliss. And the money seemed to offer this supreme version of that. But it was too much. Happiness, in the end, is far more complicated to achieve than finding a million dollars in the road.

Brain

Heart

Finders Keepers is a dope-ass book. Truly absorbing. Pick it up at any bookstore!

'A miniature serio-comedy about life in the big city . . . [that] has more than enough humor and pathos."—Jonathan Yardley, The Washington Post

FINDERS KEEPERS

THE STORY OF A MAN WHO FOUND $1 MILLION

MARK BOWDEN

AUTHOR OF
BLACK HAWK DOWN

Found a million bucks?

Avoid moral complications—send it *immediately* to FOUND Magazine!

3455 Charing Cross Rd
Ann Arbor, MI 48108

RED OWL STORES, INC.

Hopkins, Minnesota

Mailing Address: P. O. Box 1128, Minneapolis 1, Minnesota

February 7, 1956

It's the end of an era. After J. Edgar Hoover reinstates him, our bumbling friend Elmer Jacobsen lasts one more year with the F.B.I. The next peek we get of him, he's been banished from the Bureau permanently. He's moved back to Minneapolis, his hometown, and is looking for work.

Mr. Elmer L. Jacobsen
3754 N. Thomas Avenue
Minneapolis 12, Minn.

Dear Mr. Jacobsen:

After further consideration, it appears that we still have differences of opinion regarding the duties and responsibilities of a security officer employed by our Company. Until we are able to come up with a uniform definition of the security man's job, there seems little point in continuing negotiations with any applicants. Very possibly we will eventually select a far less-qualified man than we had originally intended.

We do want to thank you very sincerely for the time that you gave us. Because we were very impressed with your qualifications, we are taking the liberty of keeping your resume available. When we finally crystallize our thinking, if it appears that we have again raised our sights as to the definition of the job, I can assure you that you will again hear from us.

Yours very truly,

RED OWL STORES, INC.

Robert N. Benham

Robert N. Benham
Personnel Director

NORTHWEST AIRLINES, INC.
1885 UNIVERSITY AVENUE
ST. PAUL 1, MINNESOTA

OFFICE OF
TREASURER

June 28, 1956

Mr. Elmer L. Jacobsen
3754 N. Thomas Avenue
Minneapolis 12, Minnesota

Dear Mr. Jacobsen:

This will acknowledge receipt of your application for employment with Northwest Airlines.

As of this date we have not formalized our plans concerning our security program. We are placing your application in our files for consideration at some future date.

Yours very truly,

Wm. J. Eiden

Wm. J. Eiden

DIAMOND & JORY

T. E. DIAMOND
C. D. JORY

LAWYERS

SHELDON, IOWA

May 2, 1956

Mr. Elmer L. Jacobsen
601 Syndicate Building
Minneapolis, Minnesota

Dear Jake:

When I received your letter of March 26 last a feeling of nostalgia came over me, as I recalled the old days of the Laurens bank robbery and the subsequent trial of Kitts et al. at Mason City. Yes, I remember the great snow storm and the whole affair is still reasonably fresh in my mind, and while I received many compliments from various sources on the outcome of the trial of that case, I still believe that had it not been for your efforts and of those who collaborated with you in procuring the evidence, a different result could very well have ensued. I still recall your lying on the cold December night below the window of the room in that little restaurant in Council Bluffs on the Iowa side of the bridge, and I also recall many of your other activities in connection with that campaign resulting in sending Kitts et al. to places where they will rob banks no more. I am glad that you did what you could for Belcastro, as I always felt that he was the only "decent" one in that whole criminal outfit.

The next time I come to Minneapolis, I certainly want to have a visit with you, as I have always felt that you were the top F.B.I. man of all those whom I contacted during my incumbency in the office of the U.S. attorney.

My successor in that office is a very fine man, a good lawyer and I am really pleased to know that he is in every respect worthy of his appointment. Of course Margaret is with him, as she was with me, and she is as

- 2 -

Mr. Elmer L. Jacobsen

useful as ever. Although my successor is a Republican, he has always felt that he could not very well do without Margaret. Dorothy Sullivan of course has since married and has not been connected with the U.S. Attorney's office for several years.

I notice that you are on the staff of the Citizens League, and I take it that the League is political in character and I trust that the League will steer a course which is for the best interest of Minnesota, as well as for our country. The older I get the more I am convinced that rabid partisanship is not sufficiently interested in the matter of taking a fair inventory of issues and candidates in political campaigns. Personally, as between Stevenson and the other Democratic hopefuls, I am still for Stevenson, but I also recognize the fact that it is difficult to nominate or elect anyone for the Presidency who was known to be able at the time he ran, although some of them proved to be able men after they were installed in office. At any rate, I would much enjoy a visit with you, and I hope that some day this hope may be made real.

Sincerely,

of

DIAMOND & JORY

---

16 Sunday World-Herald,
A Omaha, Dec. 10, 1950.

Kitts' Career Like His Suits

Well-Assorted; First Trouble at 11

By John Koffend

In 33 years Kenneth Allen Kitts has sliced meat, made license plates, waited on tables, tailored suits, served in the Army, played football for a reform school, stolen cars, punched safes, burglarized homes, stores, clubhouses and filling stations.

The Federal Bureau of Investigation now believes he also withdraws bank deposits without permission. Kitts has been clapped behind bars in Des Moines while the FBI checks further.

Most of his honest trades, in fact, the paunchy, blue-eyed Dutch-Irishman learned in prisons. At liberty, he is more apt to ply his chosen profession: burglary.

Son of Minister

Saturday, in Des Moines, watching his manicure go to ruin, putting fresh wrinkles in his $175 blue suit (one of many suits), Kitts might have been pondering the convict's imponderable question:

Does crime pay?

Son of a Methodist minister, he was born in Kansas City, Mo. The family moved to South Dakota, where his father, George, bled to death after a tonsillectomy.

Looked for Trouble

While Kitts's mother, Gladys, struggled to provide food for her five kids, Kenneth, the oldest, looked around for trouble.

He was in it at 11. Juvenile authorities sent him—for incorrigibility—to the industrial school at

OMAHA PD
5-18-47

Kitts . . . last manicure?

Plankington in 1928. He stayed there seven years.

"Kenny was a good boy, a great lover of football," Superintendent Victor Hammer remembered Saturday. "He only ran away twice."

Joined Army

Paroled in 1935, Kitts wandered to Omaha and joined the Army. But in two months his record caught up with him.

From then on, Kitts was burglar. Four times the caught up with him. In seven —1938 to 1945—he did stretches, with time enough in tween only to pull the jobs sent him up again.

Since then, Kitts has manag to stay reasonably free, marry Broken Bow, Neb., girl, father on child and surround himself with plundered riches.

Found With Gun

He lived in an expensively-decorated $120-a-month apartment at 3313 Turner Boulevard and drove the best cars. Whenever Omaha police yanked him in for investigation, they found costly jewels on his fingers, a fat wallet on his hip.

Once in 1947, inside a South Omaha clubhouse after midnight, they found Kitts wearing a gun.

Kitts and his attorneys have waged a three-year battle to shrug that one off. After three jury trials and two convictions, the case is still pending before the Nebraska Supreme Court.

Two Charges

And that's not all. Down in Tennessee, authorities are waiting patiently for the day Nebraska tires of locking Kitts up. They want him for impersonating a Federal officer.

The FBI has posted two charges: that Kitts helped rob a bank at Garretson, S. D., and burglarize another at Laurens, Ia.

Unable to make his 25-thousand-dollar bond—though he has posted three more totaling the same amount—Kitts now is in jail.

Kitts, who robbed several banks and committed numerous burglaries throughout the United States, now is serving a sentence at Alcatraz penitentiary for bank robbery.

JUL 53

What does the future hold for a lifelong F.B.I. man when the F.B.I. says you're no longer wanted? Elmer eventually found work with the Northwest Indiana Crime Commission, based in Hammond, on the outskirts of Chicago. He also frequently gave speeches to civic groups and law-enforcement officials about his career with the Bureau. His loyalty never faltered; he remained forever a G-man at heart.

71st Street Liquor Store

211 SEVENTY-FIRST STREET
MIAMI BEACH, FLORIDA 33141

Telephone 865-1128

*B*ut how did Elmer's entire life files, decades later, wind up in a foul-smelling Dumpster behind an auto-glass repair shop? Did he, with great sadness, dump the boxes out one at a time? Or, more likely, did one of his children dispose of it all after he'd passed away? Perhaps a storage facility closed down and everything was discarded without a second glance. Aren't we all guaranteed the same fate—our life's great works doomed to crumble in damp basements, attics, landfills, and garbage heaps?

JAKE:
... You were snoring so peacefully, I didn't have the heart to wake you up... Anyway, I hate good-byes... As usual, you saved the re-union... for me!... Your pictures were left in my car... So here you are... Love to Bonnie...
Earl

*A*ll we can do is live. Elmer, in his later years, continued to attend F.B.I. reunions with his former colleagues. I love this note... it's such a pleasing image—Elmer "Jake" Jacobsen, lost in tranquil sleep in a motel room in Miami Beach after a weekend trading stories and reminiscing about the golden days with his old buddies.

Let us leave him here, then, and return to the stories of our own lives.

PEACE — DAVY

My mom is against Drunk Driving because last year my dad was pulled over after the fair and was charged with DWI and Child Abous because me and my sister were in the car.

Oh!... I'm sorry... I can bring u a sticker tomorrow!

That will be nice. thanks.

these photos FOUND by Don Fodness, Champaign, IL and Tom Dykas, St. Louis, MO

I can bring u a FOUND sticker tomorrow! Visit www.foundmagazine.com for more inf

WE ♥ OUR FOUND SPONSORS!!!

FOUND Magazine.
By Dogs or Traps.

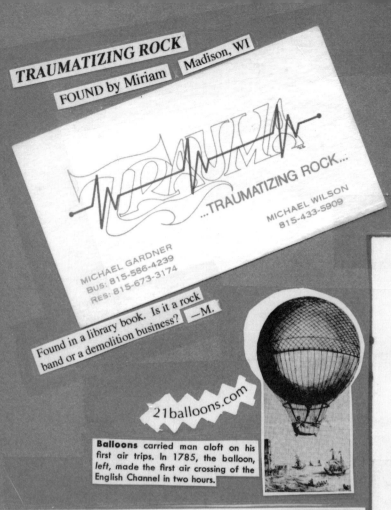

84

To become a sponsor, please drop us a line at info@foundmagazine.com!

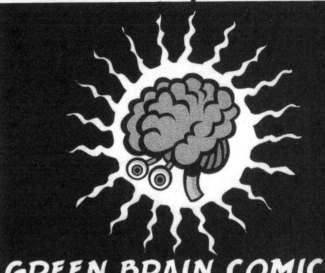

TIME FLIES   FOUND by Amy   Portland, OR

andini.org

85

NO SCRUBS   FOUND by Carlin Flora   Bowling Green, OH

- White (for the most part)
- Christian
- Drug Free
- No two fisted drinkers
- Appreciates Art
- ~~Steady Job~~
- Car
- No thugs
- Interested in long-term

This issue of FOUND Magazine was assembled to the music of The Poem Adept, Devon Sproule, and Classified.

Keep Your Silver Shined

DEVON SPROULE

The Sight of Any Bird

The Poem Adept

CLASSIFIED

www.poemadept.com

www.classifiedlive.net

www.devonsproule.com

Sonja Ohlers

Makeitawesome.com

FOUND Magazine. Steady job.

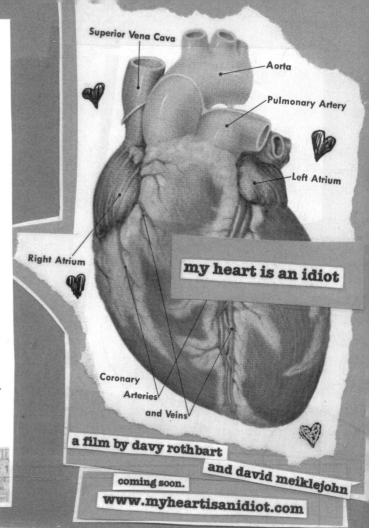

87

IRIS

The World's Leading
Independent Digital Music Distributor

www.irisdistribution.com

88

KANSAS CITY 641-661
04 JUN 2007 PM 2 T

Dear Davy,

I've been receiving the letters you've been forwarding from the kids — six so far. Thanks so much for sending them to me. Ever one it's something totally unexpected and unique. (I especially story Danielle Halinski had about her hoodie/straightjacket, sin chuckle.) If you do happen to see any of them again, I'd apprec

Byron Case, second from right, with his mother Evelyn, and, from left, *FOUND* Magazine's Peter Rothbart, David Meiklejohn, and Davy Rothbart.

After Innocence tells the dramatic and compelling story of the exonerated - innocent men wrongfully imprisoned for decades and then released after DNA evidence proved their innocence.

Focusing on the gripping stories of seven men, including a police officer, an army sergeant and a young father that were sent to prison for decades - in some cases death row - for crimes they did not commit, *After Innocence* explores the emotional journeys these men face when thrust back into society with little or no support from the system that put them behind bars.

While the public views exonerations as success stories - wrongs that have been righted - *After Innocence* shows that the human toll of wrongful imprisonment can last far longer than the sentences served, raising basic questions about human rights and society's moral obligation to the exonerated by placing a spotlight on the flaws in our criminal justice system that lead to wrongful conviction of the innocent.

After Innocence
Directed by Jessica Sanders

A REAL-LIFE "SHAWSHANK REDEMPTION"

"CHILLING!
Leaves you feeling that a new civil rights movement is urgently needed."
--Stephen Holden, The New York Times

Freedom is just the Beginning

After Innocence

Directed by Jessica Sanders

"BLISTERING"
-Carrie Rickey
The Philadelphia Inquirer

"ROUSING"
-Ella Taylor
LA Weekly

"DEVASTATING"
-Carina Cocano
The Los Angeles Times

"INSPIRING"
-David Lamble
The Bay Area Reporter

"GRIPPING"
-Michael Hastings
Metro Times

"SUSPENSEFUL"
-Harper Barnes
St. Louis Post-Dispatch

WINNER
2005 Sundance Film Festival
Special Jury Prize

After Innocence

NEW YORKER VIDEO

DVD
NYD 98507

89

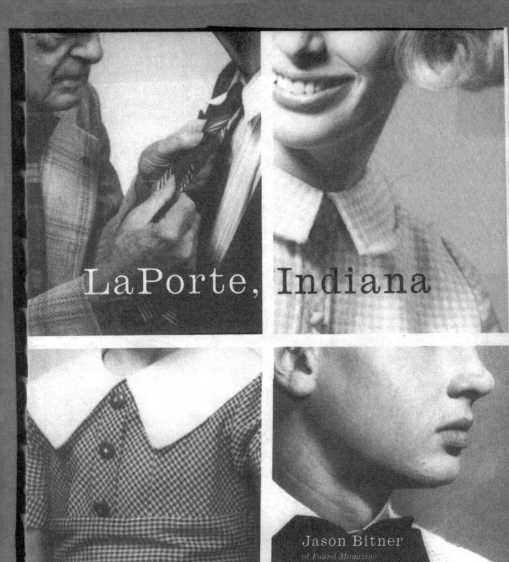

LaPorte, Indiana

Jason Bitner
of *Found Magazine*

Foreword by
Alex Kotlowitz

LaPorte, Indiana is the ultimate find!

In the attic of a small-town diner, FOUND's Jason Bitner discovered 18,000 old photographs, documenting the lives of the town's inhabitants. His favorites are shared here in this striking book.

"These are real people. The grace and dignity one sees in their faces should be a source of hope for us all."
—John Mellencamp

This American Life
from WBEZ CHICAGO.

THIS AMERICAN LIFE

SUICIDEGIRLS.com

* ♡ * redefine beauty * ✦ *

durrtyburrrd (4:23:22 PM): so what'd he say?

pleasureizyerz (4:24:46 PM): whatever. he's such an idiot. he said some shit about "ohh, i just thought it might be fun, thought that kelly might be perfect for us..."

pleasureizyerz (4:25:12 PM): ha! little does he know we've already gone there ten fucking times

durrtyburrrd (4:25:20 PM): hahahaha

Poemchild (4:25:42 PM): what do you think thought? would you be into it?

durrtyburrrd (4:26:11 PM): hell yeah! but i am in charge :-P

pleasureizyerz (4:26:24 PM): nice

pleasureizyerz (4:26:28 PM): OH

pleasureizyerz (4:26:33 PM): that reminds me

pleasureizyerz (4:26:39 PM): you will TOTALLY dig this

pleasureizyerz (4:27:32 PM): i found this site the other day

pleasureizyerz (4:29:22 PM): http://suicidegirls.com/

pleasureizyerz (4:29:30 PM): (sorry that took so long, boss came in)

pleasureizyerz (4:29:37 PM): (that was close, man)

durrtyburrrd (4:30:05 PM): what isit?

pleasureizyerz (4:30:09 PM): LOOK

durrtyburrrd (4:31:05 PM): whoa...

pleasureizyerz (4:31:11 PM): i know, right!?

pleasureizyerz (4:31:47 PM): fucking HOT girls. it's like old school pinups, but with tattooes and piercings and shit

durrtyburrrd (4:35:13 PM): damn

durrtyburrrd (4:35:16 PM): it's awesome

durrtyburrrd (4:35:21 PM): i feel like i've heard about it before

pleasureizyerz (4:35:30 PM): we should join together

pleasureizyerz (4:35:37 PM): it's like $4 a month

pleasureizyerz (4:35:58 PM): it's like myspace for adults, with naked ladies

pleasureizyerz (4:35:59 PM): :-P

durrtyburrrd (4:36:03 PM): haha, i am in!

pleasureizyerz (4:36:49 PM): shit, hang on, boss is coming back

over (as of 3/13/07)
144,103 pics!
by the time you read this we'll have even more. so, sign up now.

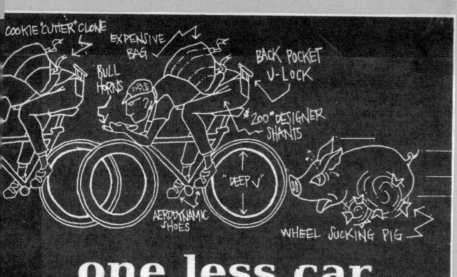

one less car

embracing tongue-in-cheek bike culture since 2005
specializing in d.i.y. bike wear
shirts, hats, stickers, buttons, etc.
www.1lesscar.com

VERSATILE   FOUND by Harry Marker
                  New York, NY

87% of the finds in the FOUND books do not appear in any issue of the magazine.

FULL BODY SENSUAL MASSAGE FOR WOMAN BY HANDSOME MASCULINE MAN CALL JONATHAN AT 212 492-5109

HI END PLASTERING TAPING AND SKIM COATING OVER 25YRS OF EXPERIENCE CALL JONATHAN AT 212 492-5109

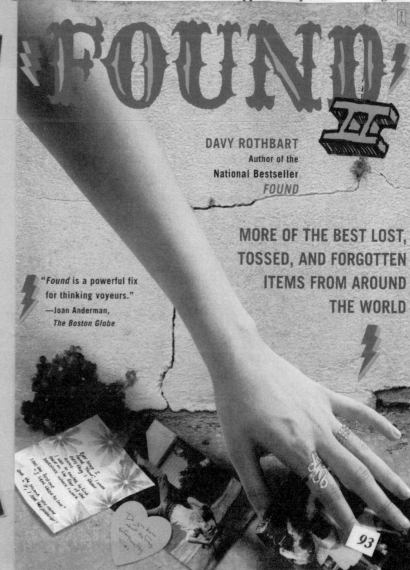

⚡FOUND⚡

SEND THIS ORDER TO

Name

Address

City   State   Zip   Country

Email

Phone

☐ **This is a gift! Please fill out the below information in case FOUND has any questions about your order**

Name   Phone   Email

All listed prices are for U.S. orders. For international orders, double the shipping price for each item.

QUANTITY	PUBLICATIONS		ITEM PRICE	TOTAL
	The First Four	The first four issues of FOUND for one price	$25	
	FOUND Issue #1	Kicked it all off.	$8 ($5 + $3 shipping)	
	FOUND Issue #2	112 pages of FOUND!	$8 ($5 + $3 shipping)	
	FOUND Issue #3	It's all about love.	$8 ($5 + $3 shipping)	
	FOUND Issue #4	Come into our world.	$8 ($5 + $3 shipping)	
	FOUND Issue #5	OUT NOW!	$8 ($5 + $3 shipping)	
	DIRTY FOUND #1	2 hardcore 4 FOUND Magazine *Must be 18+ to order*	$13 ($10 + $3 shipping)	
	DIRTY FOUND #2	2 hardcore 4 FOUND Magazine *Must be 18+ to order*	$13 ($10 + $3 shipping)	
	DIRTY FOUND #3	You're holding it now, perv.	$13 ($10 + $3 shipping)	
	FOUND Polaroid Book	A full-color limited-edition art book of the world's best FOUND Polaroids	$29 ($25 + $4 shipping)	

OTHER SHWAG

QUANTITY	PUBLICATIONS		ITEM PRICE	TOTAL
	FOUND Greeting Cards	Greet in style; set of 12	$27 ($24 + $3 shipping)	
	T Shirt	Pick your size: XS, S, M, L, XL	$15 ($12 + $3 shipping)	
	Booty CD	21 booty-thumpin' tracks. "The Booty Don't Stop!"	$12 ($9 + $3 shipping)	
	7" Vinyl Single	4 FOUND-inspired songs by Jon Langford, TRS-80, Claudine Coule, and The Victrolas	$7 ($5 + $2 shipping)	
	Bumper Sticker		$1.50 ($1 + .50 shipping)	
	1" Button		$1.50 ($1 + .50 shipping)	

send to:

Quack! Media
320 S. Main St., A
Ann Arbor, MI 48104

Allow 4-6 weeks for delivery
Questions? contact us at info@quackmedia.com
Order FOUND online at www.foundmagazine.com

TOTAL PRICE $

PAYMENT METHOD

☐ Well-concealed cash

☐ Money order

☐ Check
make payable to
Quack! Media

FOUND = the perfect gift

DIRTY FOUND

"Dirty FOUND is an anti-filth folk art that proves everybody's sex life is secretly touching."
— John Waters

FOR ADULTS ONLY
$10.00

Three

Give the gift of FOUND!!

DIRTY FOUND $10 each

FOUND magazine #1

FOUND magazine #2

FOUND magazine 3

FOUND Magazines
$5 each

$1
1" Button

FOUND magazine
Bumper Sticker $1

THE BOOTY
DON'T STOP
Booty CD $9

7" Vinyl

$5

T Shirt
$12

Your purchases are hugely appreciated and help keep the magazine going strong. Thanks for your generosity and support!!

FOUND POLAROIDS
® POLAROID ® POLAROID ® POLAROID ® POLAROID ® POLAROID ®

Polaroid book $25

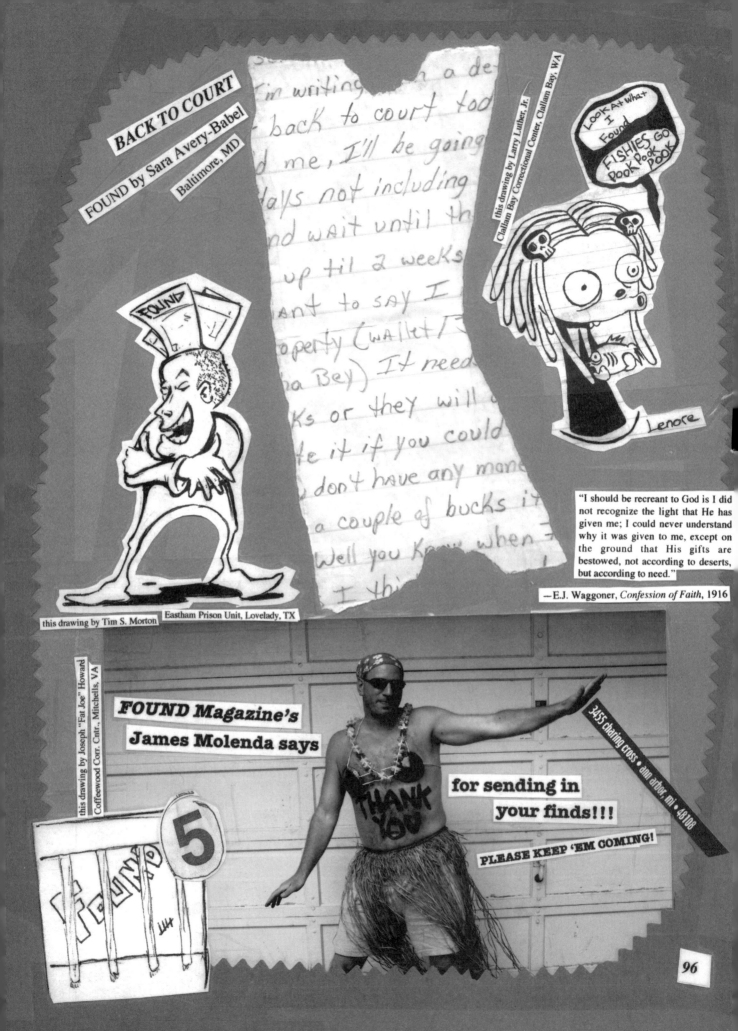

BACK TO COURT

FOUND by Sara Avery-Babel

Baltimore, MD

this drawing by Larry Luther, Jr.

Clallam Bay Correctional Center, Clallam Bay, WA

LOOK At What I Found FISHIES GO Pook Pook Pook

Lenore

this drawing by Tim S. Morton   Eastham Prison Unit, Lovelady, TX

"I should be recreant to God is I did not recognize the light that He has given me; I could never understand why it was given to me, except on the ground that His gifts are bestowed, not according to deserts, but according to need."

—E.J. Waggoner, *Confession of Faith*, 1916

this drawing by Joseph "Fat Joe" Howard

Coffeewood Corr. Cntr., Mitchells, VA

FOUND Magazine's James Molenda says

THANK YOU

for sending in your finds!!!

3455 charing cross • ann arbor, mi • 48108

PLEASE KEEP 'EM COMING!

96